TESSA WIGNEY is a writer with an Honours degree in Sociology. She is undertaking a PhD at the University of New South Wales, based at the Black Dog Institute.

KERRIE EYERS is a psychologist and teacher, and is the Publications Consultant at the Black Dog Institute. She is editor of *Tracking the Black Dog* (UNSW Press, 2006).

GORDON PARKER is Professor of Psychiatry at the University of New South Wales, and Executive Director of the Black Dog Institute. He is a mood disorders researcher with an international reputation, and authored *Dealing With Depression* (Allen & Unwin, 2004).

www.blackdoginstitute.org.au

JOURNEYS
WITH THE BLACK DOG

Inspirational stories
of bringing depression to heel

Edited by Tessa Wigney, Kerrie Eyers & Gordon Parker

ALLEN&UNWIN

First published in 2007

Allen & Unwin
83 Alexander Street
Crows Nest NSW 2065
Australia
Phone: (61 2) 8425 0100
Fax: (61 2) 9906 2218
Email: info@allenandunwin.com
Web: www.allenandunwin.com

National Library of Australia
Cataloguing-in-Publication entry:

Journeys with the black dog : inspirational stories of
   bringing depression to heel.

   Bibliography.
   ISBN 978 1 74175 264 9.

   1. Depressed persons - Biography. 2. Depression, Mental.
   I. Wigney, Tessa. II. Eyers, Kerrie. III. Parker, Gordon,
   1942- .

   616.8527

Internal design by Lisa White
Pawprint artwork by Matthew Johnstone
Set in Bembo 11.5/15 pt by Midland Typesetters, Australia
Printed in Australia by McPherson's Printing Group

10 9 8 7 6 5 4 3 2 1

Contents

10. The view from the top

Foreword

The suffering of depression is difficult to quantify, which is why story and metaphor are so valuable. While there have been many inspiring and evocative descriptions of depression (Kay Jamison's *An Unquiet Mind* (1995) and William Styron's *Darkness Visible* (1990) are key examples), most such accounts have been written by people highly prominent in their own professional lives, raising the question: Can everyone expect such positive outcomes? This book reassures us that, yes, it is possible.

The narratives in this collection arose from a writing competition organised by the Black Dog Institute, which called on people with mood disorders and their family members and friends to describe how they live with the black dog. The wealth of stories so benevolently shared contains precious insight and practical wisdom which help deepen our understanding of what is often a 'silent disease'. Individuals chart their journey with depression—describing its forerunners, its onset and impact on their lives, and, for many, their achievement of self-management, and in some cases even transcendence.

This collection captures the voices of hundreds of people aged from fourteen to over seventy, 'ordinary' at one level but at another level extraordinary in demonstrating their resilience. Many articulate that developing a mood disorder made them a 'better person'. Collectively, the grit with which these writers navigate the rocky terrain of mental illness, and the generosity with which they share their wisdom, humour and practical strategies, is motivational.

One of the great privileges of working in the mental health field is that while you see people at their worst—in terms of psychological distress—you also see people at their best. During times of mental turmoil, individuals are often open, undefended, vulnerable, yet paradoxically displaying remarkable resilience. Not only do they have to deal with a harrowing mood state, but also with the associated impairment which infiltrates their relationships with partners, friends and colleagues, as well as their capacity to work. Regrettably, this struggle commonly occurs with little external recognition or acknowledgement of the severe physical and mental anguish they are fighting, or the deep reservoirs of personal strength needed to sometimes simply face the next second, the next minute or the next day.

This collection presents a selected set of writers, in relation to the type of 'depression' they experience. Depression can range from the very physical types such as bipolar disorder and melancholia, through to the non-melancholic disorders that typically reflect the interaction between life stress and personality style. We were struck by the extent to which the writers described a particular type of depression—melancholia. Melancholia may be precipitated or augmented by stressful events but, as with other illnesses such as Parkinson's syndrome, there are also changes in the neurocircuits of the brain that have profound effects on the sufferer. During a melancholic episode, not only does the individual enter a world of intense blackness and experience a desperate sense of futility and hopelessness, but also it is a very physical state. As an individual once described, 'It is as if my brain is in a bottle beside my bed'. During such times a normally active and vital person might find it difficult to even get out of bed to wash or eat. In such near-paralysis, an individual might need someone to feed and wash them, even to take the lid off their medication bottle.

It is not always easy to know how to connect and be empathic with an individual experiencing the black dog of depression. As a consequence of the mood state, the depressed individual becomes asocial and insular, retreating from relationships and closing down communication channels, including those with their intimate partner, their family members and their friends. Dilemmas faced by those who care are obvious—to retreat or advance, to feel anger or concern, to offer advice or stay quiet, to protect or respect? The voices in this book provide some answers about how support can be offered—sometimes through practical strategies, but most simply through increasing understanding of the profoundly disabling and affective nature of the beast. It is clear from these stories that support and a sense of connection are important factors in generating resilience.

A common analogy used in the stories is that depression is like fighting a war. In the battle for sanity, there is a desperate scramble to survive the threat to self, to discover a path, and then to stay on it in an attempt to navigate through and escape from one's mood disorder. It is an unknown land-scape, often with no clear end in sight. Thus we note a consistent theme—*This too will pass*. For many, these four words have become a mantra, an integral part of the coping repertoire for both sufferer and carer. This realisation, in concert with appropriate medication, professional help and social support, can help counter the sense of profound isolation, hopelessness and negativity that is depression, reminding the individual that the state is not permanent and that they can once again regain their balanced sense of self.

Participants felt they had personally gained through writing their story. For some, this was the first public admission of having suffered depression and they were surprised to find that setting down the shape of their ordeal was therapeutic. This collection reveals there is no one correct 'way', yet taking up responsibility for one's own pathway through depression was almost universally quoted as the first stage in learning to live with the illness, including, for many, a recognition that the black dog was likely to be a companion for life. We hope you will be inspired by the fighting spirit that grounds so many of these voices.

Tessa Wigney
Kerrie Eyers
Gordon Parker

Note: For anonymity, identifying details have been changed and all writers were assigned a number. This number appears at the end of each story. All royalties from this book will go to the Black Dog Institute to support its Consumer and Community program.

Acknowledgements

We would like to express our warm gratitude to the people who helped make the writing competition, and hence this book, a reality. Hats off to our three judges, Anne Deveson, Margret Meagher and Leanne Pethick, for surmounting the huge task of selecting one winner amongst them all; our indebtedness to Sue Grdovic, our Community Project Manager, for her tireless efforts behind the scenes; and Ian Dose, our PR Manager, for his boundless energy in shaping and promoting the competition. A fond tribute to Matthew Johnstone for his inspired artwork and special thanks to Peter Bakowski, Leigh Kibby and Michael Leunig for kindly granting us permission to include their own creative gems; and the R.A. Gale Foundation for their generous donation in memory of Duncan Snelling. Finally, our warm appreciation to all six hundred and thirty-four entrants whose spirit and grace illuminate these pages: without your voices there would be no story to tell.

An invitation

No-one enters the labyrinth of depression willingly. So if you find this book in your hands, you have probably been led to it through your own pain and your own search for answers.

Or you may be a caregiver, family member or friend who is charting the peaks and troughs of life with depression as you witness the struggle of someone you love.

It is our hope that you find wisdom and inspiration in these pages—perhaps even a little humour to bring a wry smile.

This book is a map, of sorts. All the voices contained within these pages are the voices of those who have journeyed with depression, and they evoke a landscape with many reference points. Individuals share their stories, their advice, and the strategies that help to keep them well.

As you read, you may be moved to reflection, so you might like to keep pen and paper handy to record your own responses, questions, ideas and thoughts on your own journey so far.

And so we begin . . .

The traveller who looks immediately behind,
Sees only the dust of the journey.
The traveller who looks immediately in front,
Sees only the next footfall.
And the traveller who looks all around,
Sees the trail as it winds from valley to hill,
Sees the sky at day and night,
Sees the creatures, plants and land,
And sees a reflection in the stream,
And sees as far as the eye can see,
And thinks as far as the mind can dream,
And feels as deep as the heart can be.

Leigh Kibby

Truth be known, my sofa deserves an Oscar. An Oscar for the best supporting furniture in a clinically depressed episode.

211

1. The landscape of depression
Introduction to the illness

On a moonless night he comes, the epitome of malevolent darkness, stalking his prey with the endless patience of a predator, glowing yellow eyes gazing ever-watchfully at me, seeking a weakness, hypnotic eyes, second-guessing every move.

Following, ever following. Slip and he strikes, ready and willing to tear out my throat. Invincible he appears, powerful haunches, razor-like fangs framing a long muzzle. A blood-red tongue lolling in a spiteful sneer, a powerful body, black shaggy fur matted with blood, his battle trophies he wears with fierce pride.

I can never be fully rid of him, for he will always be there, lurking in the back of my mind, ready to strike . . . All I can do is lengthen the time between his attacks.

379

It is often very difficult to understand how depression feels if you have not experienced it yourself first-hand. Most people with a mental health problem will say that the experience is virtually indescribable, that the pain is incomprehensible, that there are simply no words to adequately explain it.

> This attempt to explain the nothingness, the darkness, the pain and despair seems to fall drastically short of the indescribable horror of my self-despised existence. The isolation between sadness and total despair were the parameters in which I functioned. How could anyone understand? I couldn't understand. I had become the black dog's dog. **50**

That is why metaphors are so often invoked, to provide an image that will help others move a little closer to understanding the suffering inherent in depression.

> I walked the path of emptiness with despair my loyal companion, struggling through a sopping mud pit that sucked at every morsel of energy I possessed. It was a numbness that hung over me like a stinking skin of rotting flesh, putrid and decaying with the deception of each dawning day. I loathed every breath of my existence. **119**

> I felt besieged. It felt like my head was a hellish prison, a gloomy and frightening labyrinth alive with relentless, malevolent beasts; like someone had taken out my brain and put it back in sideways. **557**

Of course, pain is a very subjective experience, no matter what the illness. But what is not often understood about depression is that the suffering goes well beyond the physical realm of insomnia, loss of appetite and low energy. Depression infiltrates your thoughts and takes over your mind. It distorts your senses, as well as your perception of the past and the future. It is a state of excruciating isolation. It fuels the most negative emotions: excessive guilt, disabling sadness and despair, and crippling self-hatred. At its worst it can hijack your most innate survival mechanism—the drive for self-preservation. To put it plainly, for most, depression is a living hell on earth.

> Deeper and deeper I fell into the black pit of hell, tumbling down in a blacker than black bottomless pit, devoid of doors or windows. Hell on earth, a living nightmare.
>
> 286

However, as these stories illustrate, in most cases the sufferer's sense of self, agency and future optimism can be restored with the right diagnosis, help, treatment, persistence, support and healing strategies.

Depression has long been an illness shrouded in a silence that has bred misunderstanding, fear and shame. Only by encouraging discussion and being willing to listen and share personal experiences can we hope to generate a discourse that will help demystify the condition. Through the richness of these stories, we gain insight into the world of suffering that is *lived depression*, an invaluable perspective that will help develop a more compassionate understanding.

Each day was like having to drag your own shadow around behind you—heavy, weighted, leaden.

129

The accounts collected here create a multi-dimensional view of the experience of depression. In piecing together these vignettes, we aim to capture the essence of what depression *feels* like in order to fully represent the depth of suffering involved in coming to terms with such a disabling, and often misunderstood, condition.

Indisputably, however, in seeking inspirational stories about how people cope with depression, a certain 'type' of depression account has been privileged. We are therefore conscious that this collection is biased towards those who describe a positive resolution to their depression story—a focus which, it could be argued, fundamentally opposes the very nature of depression itself. One writer read the tide, and swam against it:

> I am not going to be cheerful or optimistic about depression. I am not going to fabricate a worthy tale of recovery which ends with an uplifting thought. I have no story of how I am grateful that depression has given me insight. This is not an inspirational story. This is a story about why inspirational stories do not help; how they do not speak to me; how they alienate me, exclude me, tell me I do not belong in a discussion about something that is intrinsic to who I am.

There appears to be a dissonance between the possibility of redemption and recovery, and what people actually say about their experiences and their despair. What does it feel like for someone who is depressed to encounter these stories? In seeking inspirational stories, what kind of talk about depression is being asked for? It suggests the language of parables, of mythology, of the hero overcoming obstacles—a desire to see the overcoming of adversity by people like ourselves.

There is a need for discourse but there's also a need for stories which are not uplifting, which express hopelessness and what depression is actually like, stories that are not addressed to someone who is *not* depressed.

The competition framework could also be taken to exclude many other experiences of depression, for example, from those who may lack the resources, capacity or ability to articulate their experiences.

Yet it is not our intention to exclude, or silence, the darker aspects of dealing with depression. In many stories, a very bleak reality is presented. There are many harrowing elements that touch on negative aspects such as self-harm, suicide attempts, hospitalisations, relapse, and drug and alcohol abuse. Yet some of the most motivational narratives are precisely those which have highlighted the 'ugly nature of the fight' because, in their honest description of the journey from torment and attempts at self-destruction to some form of resolution, the reader gains insight into the true nature of the battle and the reservoirs of determination and strength needed.

So while we recognise the extremes of desperation within depression, we have chosen to emphasise the positive aspects of the journey towards wellbeing. For alongside each distressing testimony there emerges a reso- lution—a gathering resilience, tentative hope and growing strength—and it is the effort of moving forward that is the ultimate focus of this book. Taken as a whole, the collec- tion evidences the indomitable strength of the human spirit.

The stories we have chosen are inspiring—even if only in reassuring others that they are not alone. While we do not want to impose a concept of recovery onto the accounts, in synthesising these stories we do hope to high- light the fact that coming to terms with depression is an unfolding process and there are many avenues open to individuals trying to negotiate their way through their illness to a more mellow (albeit vigilant) adaptation.

Any victim of depression can find stories of people who fell by the wayside. It is not often that stories are told of inspirational people who recover and reclaim their lives. I have never shared my story before. It has been a closely guarded part of my life. We live in a society that still doesn't look kindly upon those who have suffered in this way. **69**

Dealing with depression raises questions, many of which remain unresolved. Sufferers do not simply have to learn how to cope with physical and psychological symptoms of the illness, but also with related issues of freedom, determin- ism, responsibility, destiny and choice.

Why? I don't deserve this! Why not? There's no answer to either question. It just is. It's up to you whether you allow it to take over your life.

162

How did it start? When will it end? Was I born this way? Or destined? I will never be the same. I have changed immeasurably.

56

The narratives that follow show that there is no one way of coping with depression. Everyone reacts to and deals with it differently—just as people have unique personalities, goals and dreams, so too do they have distinct ways of managing illness.

Depression is part of me, just like my smile, my laugh and my tears. It is all me and, like everything else about me, it is individual.

20

There's no easy answer. What works for one person may not work for another.

212

Beyond doubt, each individual has to find their own path through the pain and struggle to find their own meaning. As depression strikes at the heart of what it means to be human, understanding its meaning—whether medical, biological, social, existential, practical or spiritual—is pivotal in learning how to cope.

Depression has much more to do with the soul than with science.

411

Meaningless itself has meaning. It forces us to find, or to make, our own meanings. Lack of meaning provides the landscape in which we can seek out new truths and rediscover that which gives us purpose.

273

The level of engulfment—the extent to which depression is perceived as peripheral or dominant in people's lives and identity—is varied. Individuals often find themselves fighting to balance the split between their actual and ideal self. Some individuals cope by identifying with their illness and *learning to co-exist* with it. They come to accept it as an inherent part of themselves:

I live with it because I am alive, and it lives because I am alive. It's a strange and often amicable symbiosis. It is me. To curse this depression is to curse myself. I hope one day to be well. But for now, this is who I am.

492

Nobody asks for depression. Nobody enjoys it. Nobody wants to live with it. NOBODY uses it as an excuse to garner sympathy or hurt others. When I refer to the 'black dog', I am referring to the person I become when I am unwell. I AM the 'black dog'. I BECOME the 'black dog'. It is not a separate entity.

85

It's a part of who I am, and although it sounds strange, I wouldn't feel me without it. I have to ride it out.

127

Others manage by *separating* the condition from themselves and regarding it as something external to themselves:

Depression doesn't define who you are. You are a person coping with an illness.

176

I find it liberating to visualise this illness as a black dog that is separate from the bright, friendly, capable woman I know myself to be. I live with it by acknowledging his presence, not feeling guilty for his existence.

606

Typically, a diagnosis of depression catapults individuals into a complex trajectory of distress and adaptation. For some, diagnosis is welcomed with relief, representing a positive turning point and vital step in seeking treatment:

It was a huge relief to know that my problem was depression—not failure, weakness of character or a flawed personality.

323

For others, diagnosis is the trigger that turns their world upside down and threatens their entire self-concept and sense of coherence:

The diagnosis shocked me. I did not believe it. I'm not the sort of person who gets a mental illness. I am in control of myself. Surely the doctor has made a mistake. I don't have time to be ill.

334

A common thread that runs through these stories is one of loss and grief—loss of authentic self, agency, control, hope for the future and capacity for pleasure:

The girl in the photo, it's me. I remember her but she seems like someone I loved, but lost, and now grieve for. I want to write in the second or the third person, to isolate me from the 'dog', to give the 'dog' its own entity, to show depression and me as two separates living parallel, occupying the same space. I can't. I am the black dog, and he is me. We are a single, inseparable unity, greedily possessing and devouring each other . . . I stopped being me a long time ago and I grieve for the things the black dog has stolen from me and buried like a bone in the dirt.

380

I faded away to a shadow of my former self. It's a savage disease that destroys your very soul and the essence of your being. Depression takes away the one thing that you thought could never be taken—yourself.

385

Yet, while the overwhelming, debilitating nature of depression is explicitly portrayed in a selection of these stories, there is also a strong message of empowerment. For the majority of our writers, it is clear that being threatened with depression does not mean they have to be passive victims of their illness. Choice—in deciding to seek help, pursuing treatment, asking for support—is still an option.

> Depression is a real illness. People don't choose depression, but they can choose how to deal with it. It does not have to dictate your life. You are not your illness.
>
> 199

> If things aren't going well, don't wait around for another person to help you. Get in and help yourself. The sooner you tackle a problem, the better. The longer you leave it, the more scars you will have deep down, and these scars take a long time to heal.
>
> 54

Consistently flagged through the accounts in this book is the need for early recognition of the illness, commitment to seeking help, taking responsibility for staying well and, at all costs, maintaining belief in a positive future. Those who attest to overcoming their illness often carry an enduring sense of vulnerability and emotional sensitivity. Many are fearful of future episodes and for this reason remain vigilant.

> I am a survivor from a lifelong wrestling match with an entity that has tried to take life from me and I have emerged victorious, but cautious. I will always need to be vigilant. Judging from my family history, it is part of my make-up. I have lost too much of my life in the lacunae of

episodes and the distress between them. I don't intend to lose any more.

303

But, encouragingly, these stories illuminate a fact: the pain of depression can also heighten the capacity to experience joy:

There is an upside to depression—joy at being alive. I now have a wonderful appreciation for the good things in life. At times I feel pure exhilaration at being alive and a pulsating sensation from the very forces of life.

288

In the following chapters, we will explore the various paths used to forge a way through depression—initial confusion, disintegration, denial and escapism; reactions to diagnosis and disclosure; the role of acceptance and responsibility; and the support of others. The writers outline their coping repertoires, and describe what sustains and inspires them on the journey. We hope to provide a multifaceted foundation from which to view, and understand, the complexity of the 'parallel universe' that is depression.

Ultimately, the enduring message in these stories is one of resilience and hope.

This too will pass. This is the law of your life, the only law that you must remember.

182

To begin, six individuals tell their stories, charting their different ways of learning to identify, travel with, and finally master the black dog of depression.

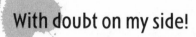

With doubt on my side!

It's a very tricky beast, that black dog. It can render your life intolerable and then tempt you with a fatal remedy, all the while robbing you of the energy to save yourself. And it achieves all this destructive mayhem in the privacy of your own mind. It turns your thoughts and emotions against you. Taming it may not be a quick process, but it is possible.

The most profound step in my recovery has been learning to doubt the veracity of my own thoughts and feelings. It was not an easy thing to come to terms with—that my inner landscape was not to be trusted. But once I could objectify my thoughts and feelings, I could allow the possibility of feeling better, that change could occur, and it was something I could build upon. The new serotonin-uptake medication was the final breakthrough I needed, but the confidence I have about staying well has more to do with insights into the nature of the illness.

Depression tricks you, it tells you lies, it is a lens that distorts your experience and it's no-holds-barred when it comes to fighting it.

It's been nearly seven years since it last blighted my life and I have revelled in every good, bad or indifferent day. Life without depression is like breathing without a flat, heavy stone on your chest and I'll do what I can to stay free of it. I believe that learning to challenge my own irrational thinking, recognising that parts of my body other than my brain can affect how I feel, and the judicious use of modern pharmacology now gives me a considerable edge.

The black dog first bit down seriously in my early twenties when I was living in hippy paradise with my husband. As despair doused me, I became inert, balled up in bed for long hours, then weeping, balled up in front of daytime TV. I went back to bed early or late, whichever best avoided sex. My feelings had heightened significance and they were all awful. I felt a sort of superior insight, I could see how pointless and futile life was—why didn't anybody else get it?

I made the sexual dysfunction a cause to seek help. I got genuine concern and sedatives at best, dismissive indifference at worst. It was the start of a pattern of reaching for help, which was a mixed bag of disappointment and relentless pessimism and tiny sparks of hope.

Over the next two decades the black dog turned up many times. While sometimes acute, my depression often tapered off to a low-level, grey numbness until I thought I was that person. Woven through all that was a sort of black romance with suicidal ideation. I planned and imagined, researched and obsessed. Only twice did I take any step towards action, and I pulled up well short of danger both times. But wanting to be dead was a regular part of my inner landscape.

Whenever I became overwhelmed with melancholy, with deep immobilising despair, my thoughts got busy making sense of it all. There was always plenty of grist for the cognitive mill as my life usually provided enough material to work with—relationship breakdowns, past hurts, an indefinable sense that there should be more. And if that wasn't enough, there was always the state of the world—plenty to despair about there. I believed I deserved to feel this way, I had this special insight into how awful it all was, there wasn't any other way to feel.

There were plenty of ideologies to reinforce my dodgy thinking. Depression is your frozen rage, or the result of a bruised self-esteem at the hands of your toxic parents, or even a past life. Just express that righteous anger, speak that truth, confront that fear, and you will be free. But those cathartic processes didn't actually work because my brain was still stuck on a broken track—shunting me back and forth on a well-worn path of gloom and self-destruction. Like the emperor's new clothes, no-one (least of all me) dared to say—maybe those feelings and thoughts are not real.

But my work with victims of domestic violence exposed me to some cognitive behavioural methods. Simple tools like affirmations (the lies you tell yourself until they are true) could peg back my destructive self-talk and slowly build a new outlook. I didn't have to wait until I felt better to try to start thinking differently—the process could work the other way around. Some small relief could be gained with distraction, the mornings felt different to the nights. Giving my right brain some air time was also beneficial, drawing stopped the bullying verbal onslaught of my left brain. So did exercise, especially weight-resistance exercise. Of course, when my blackness was at its worst, I couldn't find the energy to take any of those steps but I would get back on the horse as it abated and it gave me a small sense of control.

Finally, I got to the point where I could recognise that, despite having a good job, a caring partner and a life that was actually quite OK, the sense of doom could still be there. It wasn't a true fit, it wasn't about me at all, it wasn't even about my life. It was just something my brain was manufacturing, in the same way that a big night on the red wine or some party drugs could leave me shattered and morose the next day. It would pass, and, with appropriate new medication, I could even shut down the suicidal thinking loop.

These days I celebrate all my moods, even the bad ones. I can be normally sad and I can have just plain old contented days along with everyone else. I can be happy too, but contrary to some ill-informed opinion, freedom from depression is not about seeking constant happiness. It is the absence of that black fog that numbs the senses, muffles sound, dulls colour, divides you from your fellows and invites you to see the sense in ending it all.

It's been many years since I've needed medication. I have become a bit of a gym junkie and I no longer work in the despair industries, choices that I believe contribute to staying free of depression. But most importantly I know that 'dog' for what it is now. If its subtle workings started to bite into my inner landscape, I would ramp up all my efforts to expel it, including seeking medical help. I don't deserve that pain, no-one deserves that pain, and I won't give in to it without a fight. And I'll win because I know that its toxic whisperings are delusion.

I have doubt on my side!

The D Club

I'm the perfect party guest. Put me anywhere and I'll energise. Sit me next to the nerd and we'll be digitising computers and code, saddle me up to an artist and it'll be all art house and film noir, introduce me to a mum and we'll be gushing over the new-born. Well, until baby needs a nappy change.

Yep, I'm an energetic kind of guy. I'm into things. All things. Passion is my mantra. Be passionate, be proud. 'Tis cool. 'Tis sexy.

What's more, people respond. I ask questions. They give me answers. It's like I have a truth serum aura or something. My intuition is strong, it is real, it is Instinct. It is David Beckham.

Well now that you have my RSVP profile and we're on intimate terms, I can tell you a little secret. A kind of friend-for-life, confidante, I-trust-you-a-whole-lot secret. I'm not always the bundle of kilowatts you see before you. I'm not always the interested, interesting persona who invigorates, and who epitomises the successful young professional—the man about town who's hip, happening, sporty and fashionable.

Yep, while I sit here typing this on my new ultra-portable, carbon-coated, wireless notebook, because looks are important, I am reminded of my darkest hours. 'My achey breaky heart' hours. And I hated that song from Billy Ray Cyrus and his mullet.

Only a few months ago I finished Series 5 of 'Desperate Individuals'. It's my own spin-off from *Desperate Housewives*, except with a limited budget there were no major co-stars or Wisteria Lane—just a cast of two, with my sofa taking the supporting role.

Truth be known, my sofa deserves an Oscar. An Oscar for the best supporting furniture in a clinically depressed episode.

My sofa does what it always does when I'm alone in my depressive mindlessness. Cradles me, protects me and warms me. We've become quite acquainted over the years since my late teens. We hide from the phone together, cry together and starve together. Ain't that a shit. I have a relationship with a couple of cushions. At least they cushion me from a world I can no longer face, expectations I can no longer live up to, productivity that has left me behind.

It makes for good television. Because my life as a depressive is today's TV. It's 100 per cent reality. It's repetitive. It's boring. It's cheap. It's a mockumentary to everyone but the participant.

My sofa doesn't eat; you can tell that from the crumbs under the cushions, and with clinical depression, I'm not hungry either, so we're a perfect match. Food? My tongue is numb and I can't taste anything so why bother.

Looking back, it's hard to see when each period of depression started. That's because most depressive episodes end up being a blur; a juvenile alcoholic stupor forgetting the hours between midnight and 4 a.m., except in my mental state it's a whopping six months that are hazy and foreign.

Seconds don't exist in my world of depressive dryness. Seconds have become hours. Hours are now days. Months are lost in a timeless void of nothingness. No sleep, no interest, no energy. And it is here that life becomes its most challenging.

Don't get me wrong, I'm all for the comfortable cinema vicarious experience with stadium seating and popcorn. I just wish depression was a two-hour affair on a cold Sunday afternoon instead of the rigor-mortic torture that makes it too painful to stay in bed, but even more painful to get up.

Depression is incoherence—the death of wellbeing, direction and life. Everything aches. Everything! Your head. Your eyes. Your heart. Your soul. Your skin aches. Can you smell it? Oh yeah, ache smells and I've reeked of it. My grandmother ached. She told me just before she died of cancer. From then on I saw the ache in her eyes. Sometimes in the middle of a depressive episode, I see it in mine. To look in the mirror and see your own total despair is . . . horrendous.

Now all of this is sounding downright pessimistic and I mustn't dwell on the pain of the past. After all, I'm here to tell my story when many others are not. For I write this not to recapitulate history but to shed a little light on an illness that affects 20 per cent of adults at some time in their life.

For those of you who have been or are currently clinically depressed, welcome to the club—the members-only 'D Club'. Here's your card and welcome letter, and don't forget that we have a loyalty program. You get points for seeking help, points for talking to friends and family, and points for looking after yourself.

Now news headlines would count the economic cost of depression, which is in the billions, but from a human perspective, it's simply a hell of a lot of agony.

The good news is that public perceptions, which not long ago relegated mental illness to that of social taboo, are slowly being broken. Courage, dignity and honesty can be used to describe Western Australia's former Premier, Dr Geoff Gallop, who detailed his depression at the start of 2006. Here's a small excerpt:

> It is my difficult duty to inform you today that I am currently being treated for depression. Living with depression is a very debilitating experience, which affects different people in different ways. It has certainly affected many aspects of

my life. So much so, that I sought expert help last week. My doctors advised me that with treatment, time and rest, this illness is very curable. However, I cannot be certain how long I will need. So, in the interests of my health and my family I have decided to rethink my career. I now need that time to restore my health and wellbeing. Therefore I am announcing today my intention to resign as Premier of Western Australia.

Stories like Dr Gallop's allow more of us to talk about how depression can affect our health, jobs, families, partners and friends. It's not a sign of weakness to express our inability to function mentally. It is in fact a sign of courage, openness, sincerity and trust.

It is not unusual for those of us who are suffering from depression to feel guilty, as if we have somehow brought this illness on ourselves, that we are weak, it's all in our head, or that we're somehow protecting those around us by hiding our mental paralysis.

Truth be known, so many of us are lost in today's frenetic lifestyle that we don't see the signs of unhappiness and help-lessness in our loved ones. Sometimes it takes a meltdown to even see it in ourselves. But it is only through acknowledging mental illness that we can get treatment and start to finally feel better. Who would've thought that asking for help would be so hard?

For someone suffering from clinical depression, just to talk can be exhausting. During my last episode, I had repeating visions of falling asleep on my grandmother's lap because there I could forget the worries of my world. Memories of her gentle hand caressing the back of my neck are safe and warm. A simple gesture can mean so much.

Today, instead of my grandmother, I have dear friends who offer to cook, clean, wash and care for me. They fight my fierce independence and depression-induced silence with frequent visits and constant dialogue. Their lives haven't stopped, they don't feel burdened and they haven't moved in. They are now simply aware that I have a mental illness, and we are closer because of it.

I, too, have taken responsibility to seek assistance from qualified medical practitioners. Don't get me wrong—taking the first, second and third steps to get help from a doctor can be traumatic. It's not easy admitting that you're not coping with life. And finding a physician who you feel comfortable with, and antidepressants that work, can take time. But I am testimony that you've got to stick with it.

And so, as I sit here and start to daydream as I look out of the window, I am reminded of a recent time when I lost my ability to sing, to share in laughter, to swim, to eat, to talk, to enjoy, when waking up was just as difficult as going to bed. It's a frightful place that sends shivers up my spine.

However it's a fleeting memory, because Mr Passion, that energetic kind of guy, is back, and he doesn't have time to dwell on the past. This D Club member is in remission and it's time to party.

Blessed are the cracked

What images does the term 'black dog' conjure up for me? It makes me think of those dark pre-dawn hours when you feel so melancholy, so anguished, so alone, and that gnawing feeling of overwhelming sadness has a vice-like grip on you, like the proverbial 'dog with a bone' (apologies for the obvious dog reference), and it feels like it will never abate, regardless of what you do. (Anyone who has suffered depression would agree that things always seem worse at night.)

I have chosen to write about how I live with depression for two reasons. Firstly, I thought it would be a great way for me to reflect upon myself and the way that I deal with my mood disorder, and thus enable me to live better with it. Secondly, I wanted to share with people the way that I deal with depression in the hope that my coping strategies may be of benefit to others.

Groucho Marx once said: 'Blessed are the cracked, for they shall let in the light.' Whilst I would agree with people who say that having a mood disorder is a curse, I would also say that living with one has meant that I have had to take a long hard look at myself and reflect upon what happens in my life. I feel that this has resulted in me knowing myself better as a person than if I did not have a mood disorder. I find that I need to regularly take a step back and reflect upon my life and where I'm at in order to keep myself on track. This is certainly not an easy task, but with time, patience and treatment, it is an invaluable asset with which to maintain good mental health.

I am twenty-nine and was diagnosed with clinical depression nine years ago. A year later I was diagnosed with Bipolar I. I have two university degrees and a graduate certificate and have worked for seven of the past nine years. For the other two years, I was on the disability support pension. I have been hospitalised during both depressive and manic phases. Currently I am holding down a very responsible part-time job, own my car and am paying off my own home. For the purpose of this writing, I will discuss specifically how I survive the 'lows' as opposed to the 'highs'.

A long time ago I learned I'm better off to focus my energy on living well with depression rather than trying to fight it. Don't waste valuable time and energy trying to defy your diagnosis. Having a mood disorder is not a sign of weakness or a character flaw.

Be kind to yourself. Try hard to accept your diagnosis and work out what you need to do to co-exist with it. Whilst trying to compose a list of the strategies I use to live in harmony with the 'dog', a list of things came into my mind that one shouldn't do (even if they seem like a really good idea at the time).

Things I don't do when I'm unwell

- Put on a Nick Cave CD, press repeat, and spend hours/ days listening to it (sorry Nick).
- Not take my medication.
- Take my medication, and wash it down with Jack Daniels.
- Overindulge in recreational drugs (I rarely touch these now as I find they cause me more grief than pleasure).
- Do nothing.
- Clam up and not tell anyone how I am feeling, thus allowing that gnawing feeling to continue to tear my guts apart.
- Think I can cope on my own.
- Eat my feelings (stuffing my face is usually a sure-fire way to increase that self-loathing).

- Cut myself or attempt other modes of self-harm in an attempt to release the pent-up pain, sadness and frustration (anyone who has lived with depression will know exactly what I mean here and how difficult it is to describe this feeling).

So if these are the things I have learned (the hard way) that it is not advisable to do in order to live harmoniously with a mood disorder, then what do I do that is positive to live with depression? I have chosen to separate this into two categories—things I do when I am well (and do to hopefully stay well for as long as possible), and things I do when I feel unwell.

Things I do when I am well

- Invest energy in learning about my mood disorder—knowledge is power and the more you know about your illness, the better you are equipped to deal with things when trying to stay well or if the going gets rough.
- Surround myself with supportive people: this may include (but is not limited to) family, friends (I have found out who my real friends are when I have been unwell), others living with mood disorders that I have met along the way, my general practitioner, my mental health case worker and my psychiatrist. If you do not see a mental health professional—GET ONE!
- Have the number of the toll-free mental health helpline handy for when I do need it. This number is available from the emergency department of my local hospital, my general practitioner and my case worker. Try in

these places in your local area to find out the helpline number for your location.

🐾 Be honest with myself and others.

🐾 Laugh every day. It releases endorphins and some people even say it is a form of exercise—sounds good to me.

🐾 Stop to smell the roses—life is short, savour simple pleasures.

🐾 Exercise—they say to take it regularly, not seriously.

🐾 Get behind advocacy groups who provide support and information on mental health issues, and who do important work in helping to deconstruct the stigma surrounding mental illness that sadly remains prevalent today.

🐾 Don't say, 'I'm never going to be unwell again'. This leads to you beating yourself up badly when you do hit a bump in the road.

Things I do when I am unwell or feel that I am becoming unwell

🐾 Talk to someone. Much harder than it sounds I *know*. Picking up the phone at 3 a.m. to talk to someone is better than cutting your wrists. Toll-free helplines are available out of regular business hours. If it is during the day and not at the witching hour that I feel I need help, I get in contact with whichever of my support people seems the most appropriate at the time.

🐾 Continue taking my medication and get it reviewed by my general practitioner or psychiatrist if it no longer seems effective or other problems or symptoms arise.

🐾 If I find myself contemplating downing every pill in the house, I give all but what I need for the day to a trusted friend or relative. However, I find that if I am at this point, I really need help from a health professional. I have been admitted to hospital when feeling like this.

🐾 It is so important to make a promise to yourself that when you are well, you will continue to do all of the things you did during your recovery and that you promised yourself you would do to maintain your balanced state of mental health. If meditation, art or keeping a journal were integral in your recovery, then these are practices that you should endeavour to maintain when you are well. Think of yourself as a well-maintained motor vehicle—regular servicing hopefully means that you are not going to overheat on the highway!

These strategies are not gospel, they may not be all that the experts recommend, but they work for me. Hey, I've got battle scars—but I'm still here! If by sharing the way that I live with depression has been of some help to one other person, then it has been worth it. This exercise has certainly assisted me to reflect upon myself.

To sum it all up in one word—talk. Talking with others when you are well about depression helps others to learn about it and break down stigma. Speaking up when you are unwell will help you get the assistance you need to recover and make the most of your life.

Getting there

November 2004: I've got a problem

I'm sitting at my parents' kitchen table. Crying. Scared. This isn't the first time I've felt this way. I can't see my way through this. Every direction I turn to in my mind has a negative outcome. Every idea I have to improve my life requires energy to make changes that I simply can't muster. My parents are brilliant. Concerned and supportive, they won't allow me to spend too much time alone.

I thank God for that, and for them.

December 2004: The doctor's visit

Ashamed, stigmatised, all nerve endings on high alert, I await my appointment with the doctor. She asks gentle questions, but I don't think she needs to hear the answers. I'm one big ball of anxiety, tears and negativity, right there in her surgery. She explains the possible side-effects of antidepressants and requests to see me in two weeks. She also requests I call her at any time should I feel worse. She is an angel of hope for me. I am a lucky girl.

One week later

There is a faint buzzing in my ears and I have slowed down. I no longer feel as though all of my nerve endings are exposed. I'm experiencing very lengthy, bizarre dreams in my sleep, but apart from that I feel more stable. I take some baby steps forward, making a couple of small decisions. My world doesn't fall apart like I thought it would.

January 2005: A new job

My mother suggests I look for a job that will be easy for me to do well. She wants to set me up for success. I find one. She was right. In my normal state I could do this job standing on my head, but right now it's enough of a challenge to keep me going. I can't imagine trying to perform in a role more demanding than this one right now. I am grateful.

I begin to confide in friends carefully selected for their empathy quotient. Most are supportive, a few worry about me being on medication. I tell them I can't imagine coping without it. One, in particular, gets me up at 6 a.m. for a swim twice a week. I'm frustrated at my slower pace in the water. I can't seem to activate any adrenalin like I used to. But the water feels great and I know my body loves it, even if my mind would rather be asleep, tucked away from the world.

March 2005: Paul

Paul Hester of Crowded House takes his life. I am broken-hearted. For him and all who loved him. I wonder in what state he must have been to get to that point, but I don't wonder for too long because I am terrified of going there myself. I am doubly grateful for my friends' and family's support. It's crucial. Yet I still rarely have the energy to pick up the phone and call them. I feel guilty. I hope that they are so busy with their own lives that they don't notice. In the evenings after work, I just want to be left alone with my piano. She rides my moods with me and asks nothing in return. Reading is a joy too. I can escape from my mind into someone else's life, and some days that's a relief.

July 2005: More sunshine

A cloud seems to have lifted. I have more energy and I'm being more sociable. I am learning that I don't have to be in a perfect mood 100 per cent of the time, because my friends and family will still want to hang out with me if I'm not perfect. Though I still don't believe that any romantic partner would want me. Not with this flaw in me. Who would want to be with someone who is at risk of going on downers all the time? I'm no fun and I need a lot of sleep. Who would put up with that?

September 2005: Work and holiday

I have a new, more challenging job. I was ready for it and I know I can do it well. I no longer analyse every decision I make for possible errors. I realise that there is rarely a 100 per cent correct decision and that is OK. I head to the country for a holiday. The colours, wildlife and complete change of scenery do me good.

December 2005: My antidepressant anniversary

To my surprise, my doctor suggests I stay on the medication for one more year. She says there is a 20 to 30 per cent chance of relapse if I stop now. I am reluctant. I feel like the medication is holding me back now. I want to have more energy to do more exercise and to stay up later than 10 p.m.! But I understand her viewpoint so I agree to another six months.

I start dating again and figure that I'll just need to find a truly understanding man. Because this 'flaw' may always be a part of me. But now I am accepting it and myself for who I am. And only good can come from that.

When I'm 64

The Beatles' song 'When I'm 64' seems to connect age with decline rather than wisdom! Well, I am sixty-four and I have therefore been living with depression for a very long time. I have made many mistakes but I now believe that I have learned how to live with my black dog, for at last I have her trained, but it has been a long, slow shift in power from her to me.

I imagine there is a gene with 'Depression' written in some fancy script on one of my chromosomes. My grandfather and my mother had that gene and now in my extended family others share this gene or 'short straw'.

My early childhood may also have contributed to my depression. My mother was often depressed and, as she had no treatment, there were long periods when she was removed emotionally as I was growing up. I tried constantly to please her, but telling her I loved her, or giving her presents, or doing well at school, never seemed to cheer her up. Once I came second in my class and was praised by my teachers so I ran home to tell my mother, but she was only interested in who had come first and why I had not managed to get a higher place in class.

I slowly learned how to live with depression.

My most important lesson was when, after forty-six years, I was given a diagnosis for years of suicidal thoughts, sleepless nights, difficulties in my relationships and an unexplained lack of energy. It was a huge relief to know that my problem was depression—not failure, weakness of character, or a flawed personality. I had an illness shared by many others including some famous people like Abraham Lincoln, Virginia Woolf and Samuel Johnson.

Once I had the diagnosis I was able for the first time to seek appropriate treatment. In my case it was medication that was most helpful, though I had the usual frustrations of finding the right medication and of waiting for it to take effect. I also made the common mistake of going off the medication too early, of relapsing and of not seeking help quickly enough when the black dog was nudging me. To paraphrase Peter Cook, I have learned from my mistakes and can now repeat them almost exactly.

I found a good psychiatrist who listened to me and was very helpful, and later I got myself an understanding general practitioner. When the black dog wags her hateful tail, I now seek help immediately. The warning signs are suicidal thoughts, poor sleep patterns and, particularly, dwelling on negative ideas in the early hours of the morning.

Once, after being hospitalised, I was concerned about going back to work as a teacher. I said, 'I don't know what I will tell the students when I return to school'. One of the other patients replied, 'Tell them the truth'.

When I returned to the school I went into my class and one of the boys asked, 'What's been wrong with you?' and I answered, 'I have been in hospital for depression'. It was one of the rare lessons I gave when I had absolute silence and interest from the whole class. After the lesson, many of the students came and talked to me about their own problems and, although they were young, I felt my relationship with them had changed to a much deeper level. Recently, Geoff Gallop won respect for being open about his depression—perhaps he was even more respected for this honesty than for his successful years as Premier of Western Australia.

For many years I had used a variety of escapes as my ways of dealing with depression. When I was a child I used to daydream when I was unhappy. In these dreams I would rescue people from burning buildings or from shark attacks. I would compete in Olympic Games, out-swimming Olympian Dawn Fraser, or create great works of art.

As I grew older my escapes were more physical—I would travel or 'run away' overseas. Later, I drank alcohol or worked far too hard, and twice attempted suicide. But the 'dog' always chased me ferociously. Now I have turned to face her and she has taken a step back.

A psychologist once told me that depression is a distortion of perception, so that you see yourself and the world in a very negative way. He then added rather cynically, 'Depressed people may have the right perspective and the rest of us may be wrong'. It is true there is much sadness in the world—poverty, social injustice, war, corruption and such things can weigh you down. I remember though, after six weeks in hospital, walking in the grounds one spring day, and seeing flowers and birds and realising I had stopped looking at beautiful things for a long, long time. I have only to think of my travels to wonderful places or of the good people I know to realise that the world is a magnificent place.

I am also luckier than many others with depression as I have lived for twenty-six years with my partner, who has a good understanding and tolerance of depression. My friends know that I suffer from depression periodically and are tolerant if I withdraw from them at such times. Some are very comforting to be with even when I do feel down.

I try also to find things that give me solace. I love music and while I may choose a maudlin adagio rather than an energetic allegro when the black dog is at my side, music does help. Walking in the country or by the sea has helped me as it is difficult not to see beauty when two huge sea eagles fly above you or when a school of frenetic dolphins swims past. I have used meditation to help me relax. I try to take care of myself in all aspects of my day-to-day life.

I have also constantly sought education about depression and have tried, without being too boring, to educate others. It is a physical illness like any other and it should be treated as seriously and as without discrimination as any other illness. There are constant medical advances. Even over my lifetime, antidepressant medication has become more effective and there are new forms of treatment, such as cognitive behavioural therapy, and even experiments with the effect of light on mood. One size (or treatment) does not fit all but you learn what suits you.

I know I am fortunate and many people with depression are lonely and are quite isolated, but there are groups to join or there is individual counselling, and members of 24-hour helplines who will listen in the early hours of the morning. I try always to put something (however small) ahead of me to look forward to, a walk, a film, a day out.

So now at sixty-four I am a happy person, and when the black dog sneaks up behind me I turn and face her quickly. Suicidal thoughts, disturbed sleep patterns and excessive stress are early warning signs and I do not delay seeing my general practitioner. I know which medication helps me. I rest. I do not drink alcohol at such times and I listen to my partner and friends as they are keener observers of my moods than I am. I am not ashamed of depression and recognise it is an illness and it is treatable. There are worse things to live with than the black dog, especially now she obeys my orders. I just wish I had learned more quickly how to live with her.

Now I am older, I think of Voltaire's encouraging words:

It is true I am rather deaf, rather blind, and rather crippled;
and that this is capped by three or four atrocious infirmities,
but nothing deprives me of hope. (de Beauvoir, 1972, p. 337)

Finding a way to live with depression has been a long journey but an interesting one, and I am probably a better person now than I was when I was young. Anyhow, as I am sixty-four, I will hope for a valentine, a bottle of wine and a few more years to enjoy my life!

Learning to live, not suffer: The drugs that didn't get away

A simple poem saved my life. It wasn't a poem written by Shakespeare, Milton or Keats or even a witty rendition from Goodfellow. The disjointed words, the fractured rhyme and scribbles in the margins came from my own pen.

Time does not stop

The ticking of the clock does not stop,
nor does the passing of time.

Leave tomorrow where it belongs
and start living your life from today.
Leave that moment in time that we seek to grasp,
to hold and nurture in our hands,
to share,
to show of days that have passed.
It is a yesterday dream on today's time.
Try not to waste the hours, the minutes at hand,
because we will never get the time again.
Don't live in tomorrows,
where unsaid words and deeds dwell.
Tomorrows are only future yesterdays,
all are lost in time.
Don't sit and wait for the perfect moments,
that mystical once-only chance,
for as we wait the time flies by.
One day, an end will meet all our tomorrows,
leaving those special moments and chances with
    nowhere to go.
Use your time well and do your kindness now,
for the ticking of the clock does not stop,
nor does the passing of time.

I am no journalist or paper writer, so to do such a thing in my state of mind was quite odd. I don't really believe in miracles but me writing that day did come close in hindsight.

The actual words I wrote weren't all that poignant to anyone other than myself; it was all about a ticking clock and wasted time. I have bipolar disorder and, of course, the wasted moments were the dark spots in my daily life. I could lose whole weeks and even months to those black spots and I am sure others know what I mean.

After my initial diagnosis with the condition, the stigma of my mental health became a real issue that didn't just go away with the taking of a pill; though medication did help, and continues to help me function in our dysfunctional society. It was hard to offer an opinion only to have it slapped away with an off-hand remark about me having mental problems or that I should seek further mental help. These remarks only fuelled the decline in my health and state of being. In a hospital, fighting for my grip on the so-called normal world, I made a decision. It was nothing startling. In fact, it was a dull moment in my room of two months. If I wanted to get better, to be strong enough to wear the remarks of others, I had to understand what was happening to me. I started writing down my thoughts. At times they were erratic, dark, depressing things that seemed to stick to the end of my pen as I dragged it across the page. On rare occasions the musings were of laughter, friends and love, but all were disjointed, haphazard doodlings that seemed to bleed like a thick syrup from my mind.

The ticking clock poem, one of my first to make any real sense, helped me understand something about my illness. I didn't have to let it rule my life, the time I had, and I didn't have to live in an eternal depressed or drugged-out dumbness. There were choices open to me, many choices, and most, if not all, were beneficial to my health and future. The first was to not only take my medication but to really understand what it was doing for me. There are many views on medications but I have come to know and understand fully what I am like when I don't take them. A very tough lesson and a very tough thing to accept when I was still so young.

The poems I wrote daily helped me monitor my mood and pick up on what I considered unreasonable thoughts. Looking at a window and thinking 'It's dirty' is reasonable. Looking at the window and thinking 'I want to put my fist through it' is unreasonable. It's simple when you start to accept a few things about yourself and how your mind works.

Cognitive therapy became my next, and perhaps best, active choice. It is fine to take drugs to rectify the unhappiness and the massive mood swings—the highs and the deep lows—but it is another to learn what created them in the first place and then slowly undo all those unhelpful bits of your past. The future doesn't need to become a repeat of yesterday. The great Anthony Robbins, business and personal motivator, once said, 'The past does not equal the future' (Robbins, 2001, p. 82). Oh, how true this statement is. Every day is a new future come to life, a new start. Some of those days weren't all that bright, but I now understood that everyone has a bad day or two, so I sat back and rode with the tide for a bit and soon the brightness returned. You don't have to be UP all the time just as much as you don't have to be DOWN all the time. Most of the time I am pretty neutral, pretty much like the rest of the world's population.

After a twenty-week course in cognitive restructuring, I came face-to-face with the tiny piece of the past that became the foundation of my life. I was 'responsible' for the death of my baby brother, Scott. At the age of two, I had blamed myself for his succumbing to sudden infant death syndrome and, as a result, I cemented into my child's understanding 'I am no good'. For thirty-two years I'd lived a child's understanding of death and after twenty weeks I broke free of that belief.

After the course, I discovered it was time I rectified my past so it didn't equal my new future.

I thought the process of changing this deep thought, or core belief, as it is known, would be tantamount to raising the *Titanic*, but it turned out to be a small change of words, nothing dramatic, nothing complex. I exchange 'I am no good' for 'I'm as good as anyone else'.

There were no miracles performed that day but it was a start—I took a baby step forward and took control of my life. The new thinking helped me move from heavy suppressive medication to the new (yes, stronger) antipsychotic and antidepressant drugs. These energising and mind-clearing tablets helped me to improve even further. The elation and freedom that came with this change in outlook and actions continue to help me when those dark days trap me in bed, or turn a warm summer's week into a shadowy pit of despair. I understand the medication I must take (and, due to my condition, will have to take for the rest of my life) and I am well-equipped cognitively to deal with most stress-inducing situations, even the guy who calls me a 'mental case' whenever he drinks too much. By accepting the help of my doctor, psychiatric nurses and even other sufferers, I now live a life, rather than simply exist under the sufferance of bipolar.

There are no quick fixes or easy cures for my bipolar and I am, by no means, clear of those dark woods or the frightening dreams that haunt them. I must live partially within a set regime of medications and regular psychiatrist visits. I waste no time with my psychiatrist. We quickly review my progress openly and we try to set out a good management plan to follow. If new and better medications become available, she researches them and, if she feels they might benefit my situation, we try them. Some work, some don't, but because we talk about the whole process while it is going on, management of medications is safe and measured. I only ever stopped taking my medication once—a very dark time that I never want to visit again. I need the medication: not all bipolar patients do, but I know my own mind these days and I know what it needs. I now had two working tools to make my life better.

The poems still come. What I write now are observational in nature—my view of the world—and they are as much a monitoring tool today as they were all those years ago. I have lived with bipolar for more than twelve years and that life has been full. It isn't easy some days and my children have learned to take it easy on Daddy when he's a bit down—nice kids. I consider myself lucky; lucky to have taken those baby steps, to have followed the suggestions of those trained in mental health issues, and to have been able to help myself enough so that family and friends could build a support base around me. I think that if I put all the weight on them from the very start, I would be a very lonely person today.

It is true the ticking of the clock does not stop and nor does the passing of time, but so long as I take my medication, and keep on saying to myself that 'I am as good as anyone else', I will not die in abject depression or without saying good words to those around me.

As I look back I wonder if a miracle did happen. No-one said they had to be big and surrounded by bright lights, did they. All it took were baby steps in the right direction.

And, by the way, I don't suffer from bipolar depression any more, I have chosen to live with it instead.

At the age of sixteen, I was taken to the doctor because I was questioning the meaning of life. After reading *War and Peace, The Gulag Archipelago*, Camus' *The Existentialist* and Ionescos' *Theatre of the Absurd*, it was not really surprising.

468

2. Into the void
Confusion and chaos at onset

I felt that I had lost myself as I remembered myself to be.

595

The onset of depression is, commonly, very subtle. It can creep up over months or years—as a troubling feeling of difference, a sense of apprehension, irritability, of something 'not quite right'. In the early stages, individuals often choose to keep such disconcerting feelings to themselves. Problems remain unspoken, thus preventing the possibility of seeking help early. Many of our writers said they had no clue about what was happening and that it was only in retrospect that they recognised the pattern of behavioural, cognitive and emotional upheaval as an evolving state of depression.

I had not seen it coming because I didn't know what to look for.

423

For some, there is the immediate implosion and collapse of acute onset. For most, however, depression is like the 'unwanted visitor who arrives unannounced', unpacks bags and moves in.

Usually, there is a progressive worsening of emotions, and a pervasive sense of disconnection. Troubling feelings hover on the periphery of consciousness, clouding an individual's thoughts on waking, interrupting their work and hounding them at night. Yet the problem remains ambiguous: there is no 'template' with which to frame and understand such experiences. Most lack words with which to communicate or to describe this rising state of apprehension and sadness.

The following excerpts illustrate the chaotic confusion that is typical of the initiation into an alien landscape, and highlight some of the early warning signs that usually go unrecognised in the first episode of depression.

I'd like to say that my depression hit me like a sledgehammer, but I think the reality was that it had been creeping up on me for years.

I first experienced depression at the age of seventeen in my last year of high school. I only recognise this in retrospect. At the time I had no idea what was happening to me. Over a few weeks the world started to look grey and strangely unreal. I began to feel an overwhelming physical urge to curl up in a dark corner as if I was a hibernating animal. Things that I previously did spontaneously, like answering questions in class and eating out, made me extremely anxious.

Noise, any noise, overwhelmed me. I cried as if I was grieving but I could not explain why. It occurred to me that I might be losing my mind and I became very frightened and tried very hard to hide it from everyone, including myself. I had always believed I could do anything if I tried hard enough so I tried to talk myself out of what I was experiencing. It didn't work. I could not think properly. I felt confused and so indecisive that whether to have coffee or juice for breakfast, use the stairs or the lift, became excruciating decisions of immense importance. After a while I felt so unwell that I worried whether I actually had a malignant illness and was slowly dying. I was ashamed at how dependent I became, frightened of being alone but not comfortable being with people, relying on the patience of my boyfriend who had no idea what to do except treat me with care.

In a few months I went from top of many subjects in Year 11 to failing my final year exams. And what was even more incredible was that I didn't care. In the beginning of my second-last year of high school, I had been passionate about life, enjoying everything from politics to long distance running. I was busy, organised and able to easily prioritise what was important in my life. I had been sports captain, happily in love with my boyfriend, motivated and loving what I was studying at school, with clear and ambitious plans for future studies at university. Life was full and fantastic. And then, without anything I am aware of happening, I lost all desire, all motivation, and every-thing slipped away.

Thirty-five years later I recognise that this was my first bout of depression.

I'm fourteen years old, healthy, a little obsessed with my athletic pursuits but overall a well-adjusted kid. Then fairly suddenly the darkness moves in and I enter a new and terrifying phase of my life. I'm exhausted, not something I'm used to being. I become so tired, eating becomes a chore. I become flat and lose interest in everything and any sense of enjoyment. In fact 'flat' is only the beginning and far too soft a word for the despair that takes root. I can't seem to sleep despite crippling lethargy. Worse still, I can't switch my mind off, it nags at me incessantly.

My parents look on in their own despair—they know something is wrong, yet feel powerless. When my tears flow, as they do all too freely, I see my pain mirrored in the faces of my family. When they cry too, it becomes unbearable. Things are happening so fast, I'm no longer attending school, I'm finding it hard enough to string words together at home. I watch TV, the news and whatever else comes on. As I watch the newsreader, I'm convinced it's me that he is talking about, it's all out in the open now, I'm responsible for all the terrible things he's saying.

My dad's a school counsellor. He has some contacts and arranges an appointment with a doctor in a child and adolescent psychiatric hospital. My parents convince me to go, that these people can help, and I'm so desperate now I'd go anywhere. I'm exhausted and feel like my world is caving in around me. I am hardly able to speak, it's so intense I feel like I'm choking. I freeze up. I just can't talk apart from the occasional monosyllabic response.

The doctor is worried. He can see I'm severely depressed and wants me to come to hospital. The idea is too frightening, and we finally agree on me becoming a day patient, attending the school there. I'm started on antidepressant medication.

This is my depression: lying on my bed for days on end at the bottom of a deep, black sea pressing down on me; unable to breathe, think, move, crushed by the weight, my mind revolving around and around and around on the hopelessness, the self-hatred. Over and over the same old thoughts: 'I hate myself, I can't move, I'm worthless, I hate myself, I can't move, I'm worthless.'

The worst thing about depression, worse than not being able to get out of bed, answer the door, talk to friends, study, work, eat, move, worse than all of that, is the mind-numbing, stultifying, life-deadening boredom. While all my friends were turning their minds to career, marriage, children and hobbies, my own mind was turning to mush, the synapses staggering slowly, listlessly around and around, ploughing up the same old tedious furrow—'You're a useless, stupid, lazy waste of space'—like a raw egg rolling around in a dish; like an old drunk staggering around a lamp post trying to find the footpath to take him home.

My depression's been with me since high school. I didn't realise I had a problem; I thought I was normal, I thought everyone felt this way. I wondered how the other kids at school managed to be so cheery, to play sport, laugh with friends, study. I thought I must be weak.

169

Looking back over my life I can't remember a time when I didn't know depression. I was probably dragged out of the womb, thinking I'm not going to have much fun out here. A relative recently told me I had been 'a nervous little boy'. (Some people take great delight in telling you things you really don't want to hear, don't they?) And the nervous little boy grew into an anxious teenager who wondered why he couldn't be 'normal', why he experienced those awful hollow-inside feelings, why the past, present and future seemed to have melded into a vast nothingness that would be the rest of my life.

476

In retrospect I now realise that I lived with depression for many years, unaware of its presence. I thought it was normal to feel the way I felt—anxious and on edge all the time. Suppressing my emotions had become automatic, a way of life which I'd come to accept as normal, so peace of mind was never an option. I knew something was missing but was afraid to confront the issue in case of upsetting the status quo. *Of course, this was a cop-out for fear of facing my own feelings.*

For a long time, the black dog lurked in the shadows, hovering on the outskirts of my personality, waiting for the right opportunity to pounce. He was finally brought to my attention by way of a car crash. After being unleashed, he moved lock, stock and barrel into my home (my mind), and overtook my life like an unwelcome house guest.

All the related conditions that go hand-in-hand with depression seemed to descend upon me all at once—anxiety attacks, nausea, claustrophobia and a constant feeling of choking. (I think I was choking on the truth.) My nerve endings felt raw as the smallest sounds made me jump. I suffered sleep deprivation caused by hyper-vigilance as my brain was on full alert 24/7 and there seemed no escape from the all-consuming fear that had become my life. I thought I was losing my mind and felt completely alone—except for *him*!

Whenever there's any sort of crisis in our house, Mum cooks. Tonight, our plates are loaded with strands of slimy pre-cooked chicken, canned peas, lettuce, beetroot, chunks of boiled egg and quivering dollops of mayonnaise.

'I'll never eat all this,' Dad complains. But he does, and when he's finished he bashes the cutlery into the centre of his plate. 'Can I get a cuppa tea?' he asks me.

I make him and Mum tea. I dunk Mum's tea bag in once and sit it on the edge of the sink. I shovel a teaspoon of sugar into Dad's mug, leaving the tea bag in, and give it a quick stir. Later on, he will turn the page of his magazine and squeeze the excess water out of the tea bag, leaving it to dry on the teaspoon like an abandoned life-jacket.

After I have done this, I shuffle off to my bedroom.

Even though I am twenty-four, Mum comes to tuck me in, anxiously asking whether I have enough blankets and do I want a hot water bottle because the nights are still quite cool and she doesn't want me to wake up in the middle of the night feeling cold . . . I lie beneath rows of leering teddy bears and peeling posters of out-of-date pop stars, relics from my adolescence. It's been a long time since I have lived at home.

I can hear Mum and Dad's voices, low and urgent.

'Maybe she should go to hospital,' Dad's saying, emphasising the 'should'. Mum's rubber gloves creak and snap as she fills the sink with water for the dishes. It's comforting.

I don't have real sleeps anymore. I fall into a synthetic oblivion aided by the orange sedative Mum doles out every night after dinner. In this sleep, my limbs are sedentary and I don't dream. I always hope I'll wake up and everything will be normal again. Only that never happens.

526

It started for me with sleep problems. Tired and wired at 4 a.m., falling deep into sleep at 6.30, just when my normal work day started. I had no idea about 'early morning waking' being a symptom. I had headaches and neck and shoulder pain. For a mental illness, it was pretty damn physical. I was removed, like I was trapped in a Perspex™ box a bit shorter than me. People would greet me, and I would will myself to smile, but my face did not respond. As I sat with friends over coffee I watched them from five metres away, as if my mind was standing in the corner while my body sat across the table unresponsive. I felt like a cyborg on *Star Trek* trying to understand humour and mimic real people's facial expressions.

I sat at my desk and the numbers and words I used as a financial controller may as well have been ancient Sanskrit, for all the sense they made. Work piled up. Social engagements fell by the wayside. I thought I had woken up with brain damage or a tumour. I felt stupid and slowed and my temperament warped and changed with my confusion and lack of sleep. I longed for the flu, so I could stay in bed. Everything I wanted in life was right there under that blanket. I didn't understand. There were no solutions for the simplest of problems, and there was no escape from the circling pack of thoughts.

I had weights on my head, a slouching posture and tunnel vision. I ran into things, I had no sense of my own boundaries. I was bruised all over. My hearing was magnified beyond belief. A sniffing man on the other end of a train carriage could have led me to murder. It took me months to recognise these symptoms for what they were.

My particular black dog was a sneaky little fellow, an unassuming mongrel who didn't tread a clear path to my door. Rather, he snuck around the back when no-one was looking, and, under the auspices of an anxiety disorder, life stress and hormonal changes, he slipped through the side door. By the time I realised he was there, not only was he in like Flynn but he'd taken up residence on the couch!

I realise now, looking back, that I was living with the 'grey dog' for many years. During that time, I felt a sense of 'nothingness'. I had thoughts such as, 'Life is meant to be hard', 'I just have to put up with it' and 'What other choice do I have?' Increasingly, I had a feeling of hopelessness.

Cunningly, the grey dog began to intrude more into my life. I started to forget what 'happiness' was meant to feel like. I was in denial that anything was wrong. I realise, now, that I probably had to go through depression to get to where I am now.

The first tangible sign of the black dog's arrival was when I started waking up most mornings between 1 a.m. and 4 a.m., and worrying until daylight arrived. I soon became utterly exhausted, physically, mentally and emotionally. I somehow continued to work full-time though, probably because of my drummed-in work ethic. But to do this, I became a recluse of an evening, and every weekend, trying in vain to catch up on some sleep.

I increasingly avoided interactions with others, including phone contact, as any conversation seemed to deplete my already low energy. Increasingly, I was becoming enormously hurt by the remarks of others. Even the most minor criticisms left me reeling. I soon started 'losing it' at work. I'd often race away to cry somewhere in private. At times my work colleagues discovered me, and so I'd blame it on 'headaches', which I frequently had anyway.

When the black dog lurks, we are hesitant, indecisive, humourless and maudlin. We have headaches, our vision and perspective is blurred. We are tired, listless and bumbling, with aching shoulders, legs and arms, as well as being a pain in the neck to those around us. On those days when the dark eyes of the black dog burn with a smouldering intensity, suicidal thoughts grow strong.

It all started a few years ago. I'm not sure of the exact day or month. Depression isn't the kind of illness that you wake up one morning and suddenly decide that you have it. It sort of creeps up on you whilst you aren't looking. Slowly and gradually increasing in intensity as the hours, days, weeks and months crawl by. Depression never really crossed my mind at first. I mean, I was only seventeen years old at the time. I didn't know much about depression back then, but I didn't think it could affect someone so young—and especially not me.

I was first diagnosed with depression in my last year at high school. I remember my graduation week clearly. While all the other students were celebrating and looking forward to the future, I was walking around in my own little dark cloud. After our final school exams, most of my classmates headed north to party and have fun. I spent the weeks after graduation running away from home and planning how I was going to end my life.

My metaphor for depression is a murky room, no windows and only one exit, locked from the other side. The room is stark and bare of furniture except for a gas fire that doesn't warm so much as leave a chill clamminess behind as it gorges on the air and leaves me to breathe in my own despair and smell my own fear.

Hell is not 'other people'. For me, it's being sealed in with my sad morbid self and no other person, no ideas, no books, no music, nothing to distract me from my preoccupation with feelings of doom. I have malaise in my body and self-loathing in my heart.

I like my own company as long as I can reach out into the world and be part of it. Depression makes me an island in a desolate sea. No-one can thrive in this situation and be whole.

Fortunately, it hasn't been as bad as this for a long time. Now it's like walking in a dark street with my melancholy double until daylight comes and the doppelgänger fades away.

From childhood I've always felt 'inappropriate'. I would be ecstatic over trifles and the world would glow and I would expand outwards, but at other times I would shrivel inwards towards the gloom gathering in me. When I was eighteen I had my first 'breakdown', one of my life's lowest ebbs. I was metaphorically shut in a tomb in an ever-deepening gloom, where 'only death could reach me', as I morbidly wrote then. I bounced back but had recurrent attacks till, at twenty-eight, I was diagnosed with depression, and given medication.

Depression. The dark room where
negatives are developed.

380

3. The slippery slope
Sinking into depression

> All people should be aware that the possibility is there for this to happen to any one of them.
>

Depression is like a game of snakes and ladders. It feels like your fate can turn on the roll of the dice. You might scale ladders in a scramble to get on top, only to find yourself knocked down, on a slippery path straight back to the bottom rung.

Despite the signs and mounting feelings of impending breakdown, nobody at first fully believes that they have depression, that their lives are unravelling beyond their control. And so they soldier on. They keep moments of collapse firmly relegated to toilet cubicles or behind bedroom doors. They take sick days or plan a holiday. They become adept at fashioning excuses for their growing withdrawal and distance. They start avoiding phone calls. Above all, they keep their mask of normality firmly in place.

So confronting is it to face the truth that something is wrong that sufferers tend to ignore, deny and distract, in the fervent hope that things will get better and that they will eventually return to a more balanced state of mind.

> Unfortunately, unchecked depression usually only gets worse, leaving the fundamental question: How does one flee oneself? 350

This chapter focuses on the lived experience of depression—what it feels, smells and tastes like. In our analysis of the stories, there was a striking consistency in the way people described their depression. The most common metaphors were of being trapped in a dark pit or windowless room; feeling as if walking through fog with a cloud constantly over their head; and fighting a separate entity, a malevolent presence that was attempting to take over their soul.

Depression's signature is the experience of extreme isolation and loss. The stories that follow starkly illustrate this, and convey some sense of the pain endured by so many.

Confusion drags my thoughts in ever-tightening circles. The routine of my life is swept away, so much flotsam in swirling currents of sadness and grief, overwhelming in their intensity. It is familiar, this undertow that heralds a downward spiral. Not welcome but accepted. I know well the process.

Reality blurs. Imagination sharpens to a blade, slicing away optimism, hope and joy. It fillets dreams, hacks into the veins of inadequacy and self-loathing. The pitch-dark maw of depression welcomes me back with a fierce embrace, an overprotective mother clutching her child who arrives home from school camp. This embrace contains little comfort. Instead, it squeezes and stifles, smothering the passion for the extraordinary as well as ordinary delights seen, felt, heard and tasted.

All senses are dulled to everything except the darkness rushing to greet me. Gone is any pleasure in the sight of a blue organza sky smeared with tufts of white angora.

Yesterday, the garden was a haven for getting close to nature, a source of peaceful productivity. Today it fends for itself against the harsh climate of drought. The 'To do' list grows. Mundane tasks, that have brought some measure of structure to waking hours, slide and fall away unnoticed while a morass of emotions cling-wraps my body and mind. Simple pleasures are lost amidst ironstone days and sleepless nights, the dark hours filled with nameless phantoms, which clamp me, writhing, to the bed with twisted sheets.

Like a victim of recent summer storms, I lie by the roadside called Life, battered, broken, roots wrenched from the earth, bark stripped to tatters, revealing the tender, mutant core of my being. Even the promise of my grandchildren's smiles and laughter lacks the enticement to make me get in the car, drive twelve minutes, and visit. I am poor company and will shelter two free spirits from my lethargy. Perhaps tomorrow, or perhaps not.

Showing up for work, day after day, becomes a trial, a marathon of endurance. There is no celebrating my tenacity and bloody-mindedness to get through eight hours until I can remove the mask of professional amiability. Frequent visits to the toilet, to cry for no reason, are yet to be noticed. Though the truth will come when the mask falters, revealing the shadows reflected in my eyes.

I should consider myself lucky that I am still able to participate in a day job. Others cannot, as I could not have done eleven years ago. Soon, if I don't take preventative measures, the pull of despair will be too great, the will to fight bludgeoned to extinction by apathy.

458

People with depression swim in the same stream. They paddle hard for happy days and dry land. The illness can strike like a stingray, leaving an agonising barb without regard for the victim. It can invade as stealthily as the flu, coming in with the wind and staying as long as it desires. While it may not kill like cancer, it remains a life stealer. Depression lies behind the eyes of the sufferer, trapped in the brain.

562

Nothing can compare with the bite of the black dog. It is indescribable and unimaginable to those who have not felt the savagery behind its bite or to those who have not witnessed the terror of the attack on their loved ones or friends. You cannot comprehend unless you have 'felt' or 'seen' the teeth marks first-hand or shared in the experience of the pain and sorrow those wounds leave behind.

I was seventeen when the black dog first started to stalk me. It picked up on the scent of fear, apprehension, loneliness and despair emanating from a friendless, gawky teenager fresh out of high school. I felt alone, unloved, unwanted and scared. The perfect formula for the black dog to make a meal out of. Twenty-four years later and that wretched mutt still finds a bone or two in my life to gnaw on.

I still bear the scars of the razor's edge, one of the many wounds encountered during countless 'dog fights' I've had over the years. The inner wounds are far uglier but, thankfully, no-one sees them but me. However, I am certain that all of you who have been bitten bear your own scars, seen and unseen. I know you can relate. Me writing this and you reading it undoubtedly proves one thing—we are fighters! We have already learnt, or are willing to learn, how to live with depression.

Learning to live with depression is, in essence, the same as learning to live with any chronic, debilitating illness. There are, however, a few key differences that make the experience of depression uniquely excruciating for the sufferer. First, depression is an illness of seclusion, of inaccessibility, which forces us so far inside ourselves that we are often rendered incapable of connection.

Depression does not possess the specificity and the tangibility of an ulcer or broken leg. The darkness is silent and invisible to observers, making sympathy and identification more difficult. Indeed, many depressives yearn for something tangibly horrific and external that others can observe.

471

I have looked into his eyes and swum in the depths of his darkness. These depths that we go into are as deep as the ocean and, just like the ocean, the deeper we go down, the darker it becomes. So it is with our depression. On the ocean surface we can see things clearly, but as we dive deeper, our ability to see diminishes. Eventually you can dive so deep that all light is shut out.

Keep this in mind next time you are dragged down by the currents of life. If you are in the depths of your depression, know that your ability to see your life and its potential has greatly diminished. Do not be fooled by these depths—the depths are murky, there is barely any light, and your ability to see and negotiate what is around and in front of you is affected.

402

I used to wake each morning with the sinking realisation that a) I was still alive, and b) I still felt besieged. Needless to say, I wasn't exactly bounding out of bed—more like hauling myself from it, and then dutifully engaging in my daily battle against unwanted thoughts and feelings, which took an inordinate amount of energy. I was almost constantly sad, but, worse, I felt total despair—because no matter what I did, there seemed to be no way out. Then there was the thinking: the continuous pondering, analysing, self-criticising, yammering and yearning. It was constant, chaotic and exhausting.

Depression was like that for me. It seemed inescapable. It felt like my head was a hellish prison, a gloomy and frightening labyrinth alive with relentless, malevolent beasts. It was like someone had taken out my brain and put it back in sideways, or as if the entire physical contents of my head had been pushed to the front, creating an unbearable, gooey pressure.

For some of us depression is the default human condition and laughter, joy, optimism and confidence are fleeting aberrations. There are, of course, a multitude of things that can bring on depression: the general state of the world, politics, threats to our personal freedoms and our way of life, economic rationalism, inflation, the stock market, our health, being tied to work that we feel is beneath us, relationship traumas, the treadmill of mortgages and debt, dealing with the death of someone we knew and loved, loss of libido, racial and religious intolerance, the weather, the fortunes of our sporting teams, the nation's international image and reputation, and the plethora of other disappointments and disillusionments with career, love and life. And these things become cumulative. As Michael Leunig says:

> A most depressing thing occurs
> But no one minds and no one stirs
> Which means you've ended up with two
> Depressing things depressing you.

Reflections on past mistakes, chances missed, family neglected, friends wounded, money squandered, gauche responses and pompous poses all metamorphose into a malaise of the spirit. A paralysis of action results from our profound disappointment with the self we see and the puny specimen that we believe we have become. We are not the fairest of them all! We are not the person we once thought we were and will never become the person we aspired to be.

150

My bed is my sanctuary, as is the bedroom. With blinds drawn and door closed, my extreme sensitivity to light and noise is at least reduced, allowing me to slumber more peacefully—for this is my greatest desire—to go to sleep and never wake up. But even in sleep, irrational, negative, guilty, self-admonishing and paranoid thoughts still haunt me. These thoughts swirl, churn, clutter and confuse my mind. Bad memories take control, chasing me further down the spirally whirlpool that is depression.

21

Depression begins, for me, in winter. It starts slowly and insidiously, the greyness of my mood matching that of the sky: but when the clouds finally roll away for me, I stare at the baking blue sky of summer—and I have missed spring.

I've been depressed before, though never so severely, but this time, somehow, I miss the early warning signs. We are in our fourth year of drought, money is tight, it is getting harder and harder to feed our stock and sow our crops. It is perhaps understandable that the early signs of depression are attributed to anxiety about the situation and the future. But the depression increases—and the black dog is in control.

By the time I seek help I am waking up in the early hours of each morning and lying awake worrying. I have stopped answering the phone or talking to friends and family if I can possibly avoid it, and I am increasingly disorganised in my work. I start doing one thing, then another, then a third—then find it all too hard and sit at the computer playing endless games of Solitaire. More worrying in terms of health is my drinking—I have one drink before dinner which makes me feel less sad, then a second which does the same; so I have a third and fourth. Unfortunately, they have the opposite effect and so I keep on drinking, hoping to recapture that first euphoria, but instead descending deeper into depression, either that night or in the early hours of the morning.

My mood becomes lower and lower—I take no pleasure in the things I loved before, like playing with my grandchildren, socialising with friends and family, and working in community groups. It is as though there is a glass barrier separating me from those I love and care for—I can see them and hear them but I cannot share their laughter, or even their tears.

I don't remember the exact moment I realised I was depressed. Most days I would cry, sometimes I would fantasise about killing myself, and other days I would stare out the window, waiting for sometime to happen, for someone to save me, for things to change. It was a slow falling into myself, a secret withdrawal from life too subtle for most people to notice.

After months of helpless rage, stifling immobility, emptiness and inexplicable feelings of grief and loss, I realised I was in trouble and needed help. Although part of me resists this call to action, I felt that my life depended on it. I made a call to a therapist. As Lao-tzu said, 'A journey of a thousand miles begins with a single step'.

We became adept at reading her
moods—unmade beds (depressed);
wearing socks with sandals
(very depressed); donning her brown
beanie (possibly suicidal).

4. At the edge
Lure of the dark sirens

Depression is a disease. It's not terminal—it doesn't have to be fatal.

82

As depression worsens and tightens its hold, thinking can become more irrational, self-perception more distorted until it feels like there is no escape from the bombardment of tormenting thoughts. Compounded by the extreme weariness brought on by lack of sleep, incessant worry, increasing isolation and the incommunicable nature of the experience, the suffering can soon feel unendurable. Hope for a peaceful future appears as a distant landmark on a bleak horizon.

Often I've looked down the years ahead and seen only darkness and hopelessness. There was seemingly nothing to live for, nothing worth stirring for—nothing . . .

241

With the mind and senses in an increasingly anguished state, individuals begin to convince themselves they have become an overwhelming burden to those they care about. It is not uncommon for individuals with unrecognised or untreated depression to search for ways to stop the pain. They long for something that can silence the brutal force of depression's attack and grant a moment of peace.

As anyone who has depression knows, just being here and surviving another day is coping. Anything more than that is just short of a miracle.
293

My entire world is collapsing and there is nothing I, or anyone else can do to prevent it. It feels like life is being leeched out of me.
180

There are some who seek to numb the all-consuming anguish by distracting themselves—keeping frantically busy in an attempt to escape themselves in overwork and a full social calendar. Others turn to more destructive behaviours, such as self-medicating with alcohol or illicit drugs.

I took anything I could find to escape the pain and reality of the intense darkness I was feeling inside.
253

This is part of the pattern of untreated depression. Before seeking help for symptoms, people can find themselves cata-pulted onto different trajectories of suppression, escapism and self-harm. Such destructive behaviour is a clear warning sign and should be taken seriously before it escalates out of control.

Constant thoughts about death and active suicide ideation are common features of depression. Many of our writers admitted to contemplating suicide. *All* make the point, however, that it is not that they wanted to die but that they simply could no longer bear to live. In the face of such unabating pain, a seductive choice looms.

The loving arms of oblivion seemed the only way out.

This is depression at its most powerful: at its worst, it can be lethal—a tragic reality for many families. Yet those who die from this harrowing choice are surely casualties of an illness. Perhaps it is more accurate to say a person 'died from depression' than to focus on the act of self-harm.

The stories that follow depict how it is possible to be driven to the edge of endurance, where despair, exhaustion and confusion tempt the sufferer to consider suicide.

It's as if I'm possessed by something sinister. It's like having a little man sitting on your shoulder, whispering in your ear constantly how worthless you are.

As our writers attest, however, those that hit rock bottom reached a vital turning point that led to a more positive path of help-seeking and change. Once assistance is sought for such damaging thoughts, instincts and behaviour, preoccupation with death starts to lift. Thus, for those in a stage of utter despair, it is vital to remember:

Feelings pass, so don't act on them.

I am scared to write this piece for three reasons . . .

Number one. How can I possibly write about my experience with depression, my time spent desperately trying to get air into a room with no windows and trying to reconnect to a world where everyone had a hand to hold but me, and make it uplifting or optimistic? How can this possibly be reader-friendly when I would never dare to invite my worst enemy (but maybe my ex-boyfriend's new girlfriend) to experience that darkness?

Number two. I am an intelligent woman, yet there is no way I have the words in my vocabulary (or on my computer thesaurus) to do justice to the utter desperation that suffocated me during that time. Nothing can describe how bloody hard it was.

Number three. This is why I am truly frightened and have put off writing this for days now. To write something really good, really expressive, really honest, means taking myself back to a place I never want to go to again. I am honestly scared that if I go there I will not come back. Maybe the first time was a fluke. Maybe I am doomed to sleep forever with that black dog snoozing at the foot of my bed. Maybe sanity just doesn't 'become' me.

So how to deal with that black dog, constantly panting, demanding attention, and yet sucking anything you have to give straight out of you? The best I could do was force myself to place a slice of bread in the toaster and then reluctantly nibble on the crust. Except sometimes when it burnt I would burst into tears and fall to the ground in hysterics, much the same as a two-year-old does in an icecream shop if the rainbow-coloured bubblegum-flavoured double cone they had their heart set on is forbidden. Except with way more desperation and without actually wanting anyone's help or anything to get better.

I wouldn't recommend any of my methods for coping. Fluorescent drugs bought from dodgy bouncers washed down with vodka. Washed down with vodka while chain-smoking cigarettes. Chain-smoking cigarettes while wearing a push-up bra. And doing all of the above while letting a man I barely know take me home.

Then there was the dirty kitchen knife in the top drawer of my bedside table. I used to wear a lot of jewellery during those days. Not meaningful, rare droplets of gold, but cheap hyper-coloured beads, found everywhere from under my little sister's bunk bed to inside those red plastic balls you get if you put twenty cents into a toy machine at the bowling alley. I never realised it then, but the more I draped around my neck and the brighter they were, the worse I was feeling. The proverbial cover-up. Those beads were pretty much all I had since my outgoing happy personality façade had long gone out the window.

Then there were the bracelets. Circles of glitter, shine and vibrance. They had a more practical use. No-one would see my wrists. I would put them on every morning without fail. Every morning so those around me wouldn't need to be confronted by what they knew was happening every night. I eventually started to sleep with them on. No-one would see them now— including me.

Sleeping was my only escape. It became this faraway place where I didn't have to hear my dad and my sisters and my best friend giving me a pep talk to keep me going. It was a place where I didn't have to pretend I was giving myself that pep talk. It was a place where I could relax with the idea that I really didn't want to keep going, and where I didn't need to hurt people's feelings or feel ashamed when I thought it.

I remember waking up one stinking hot February morning the happiest I'd been. I had realised that things didn't need to keep going on like they had. I didn't need to pretend anymore or try to fight. I remember rolling over and telling my boyfriend that I had found the answer. I wouldn't have to worry about uni or getting a job or the annoying girl that was following him around anymore. He wouldn't even have to worry about me anymore. If I ended it all now, things would never be hard again.

The next morning the doctor put some gauze on my left wrist and handed me a box of antidepressants.

It's funny, because just last week someone told me I was too loud to have ever been depressed. The same person told my friend that I was 'too pretty'. It's scary to think how many people I have fooled.

During that time, I had no hope. Hope was something which came more after the fact. Hope came when after three months of being practically bedridden (except to use the toilet and to crawl into the kitchen for more ice blocks) I sat in the lounge room and stayed awake until early evening. Hope came when, after not walking further than the mailbox for months, I walked down the street. Dad drove to the end of the street to pick me up. And on the drive home I felt prouder than the day I finished Year 12 or got my first job or graduated from uni.

And then slowly I came back to life. I didn't return to my old one though. I didn't magically rewind three years to the girl I was before I became sick. The one who talked a lot about nothing, who thrived on the adrenalin of sneaking into bars, and who was obsessed with football players she barely knew. Nor would I have wanted to.

I returned as a young adult who has been through hell. Who still cries when she thinks back to those times and that darkness and that knife. Who is floundering now while trying to proof-read this. But who can believe in herself just that little bit more. Who doesn't have to turn around and go back home when she realises she isn't wearing bracelets covering both of her wrists. Who, when the toast burns, doesn't want to end it all.

And who, on most days, is bloody happy that she never did.

Everyone needs to understand that suicidal thoughts are not controllable, or thought of by choice, nor is the act one of cowardice or selfishness, but one of desperation and desire to be rid of the pain and overwhelming, all-consuming torture that is depression. When in the depths of depression, there is no escape, for you cannot escape yourself. Irrational beliefs when depressed lead us to believe that we would be doing our family and friends a favour by removing ourselves from their lives; removing the worrying, demanding burden that we become when depressed. Like everyone else who suffers from clinical, deep-seated, overwhelming, all-encompassing depression, I feared my next spiral down into the pit of despair from which there seemed no return. Fortunately, because of coping mechanisms I have put in place, the severity of my depressive episodes has been significantly reduced.

Dear God, I have been so depressed I have begged and prayed for my life to end on perhaps four or five occasions. During these times, I have despaired at my own inability, despite adequate means and knowledge, to take my own life. I know that at some time in the future, perhaps as the winter approaches, this terrible violent thought will insidiously creep back into my being, and I must be vigilant to ward it off, to fight again when I am at my most weak, tired and vulnerable. I can now recognise this thinking when it permeates my thoughts and threatens my existence, my amazing, wonderful life. THIS IS THE TIME TO CALL IN REINFORCEMENTS!!!

Overmatched

Here I go again,
Another fifteen-rounder
With Churchill's 'Black Dog',
Who hasn't lost too many,
And me, well I haven't
Won too many yet,
But I'm in there fighting,
With vodka and Lou Reed
Who's singing about a perfect day,
And I'm writing these words,
Trying to fight my way out

And getting in a few good shots
Until the black dog retreats
To his corner where he waits.
He is good at waiting,
he knows how to pace a fight,
he's got all the big scalps—
Hemingway, Plath, Monroe, Cobain and
Countless thousands of
Stumblebums like me,
And he'll get me one day,
I know that,
And when I go down for the last time,
I'll see those lights,
The distant lights of promise
Never fulfilled, but even then
I'll ask myself
Was I ever a contender?

I wrote that poem one morning when there seemed to be no point in being alive. All I wanted to do was go back to bed, pull the covers over my head and wallow in misery. Instead I forced myself to sit at my desk and start to write. Something. Anything. An hour later, I had finished my first draft, put the vodka away and felt ready to take on anything the world could throw at me.

Ah, if only it was always that easy. Feeling bad, so bad you want to die? Then write a poem about feeling bad and you'll feel a whole lot better. Unfortunately, it rarely works that way. The black dog is a formidable foe and is used to getting his way. He doesn't like it when you try to crawl your way out of the black hole. (I call it a black hole because, like Professor Stephen Hawking's discovery, it draws all the life, all the vitality out of the sufferer.)

Like many depressives I turned to alcohol and illicit drugs, anything to chase away those ugly feelings. And alcohol works. For a while. Then it turns on you, like the true depressant it is, and puts you back where you started. The secret I've found is moderation, knowing how much you need to give yourself that lift. Winston Churchill knew this. He always started the day with a small whiskey and kept a glass on his desk. Of course this approach is not one I recommend—it takes iron discipline to avoid sinking into alcoholism—but if having a drink stops you from walking in front of a train, then open that bottle. As for illicit drugs, they don't work. Simple as that. It's been more than twenty-five years since I've had even a joint, and, despite temptations, I've always refused and take a certain pride in my discipline. 476

Imagine, if you will, a dark and cavernous space filled with shadows and screeching noises. Imagine being alone in this space with no light able to penetrate. Then imagine voices in your ear, telling you this is the only way life can be for you, that darkness is all that is left, that you are dead inside, so you may as well be on the outside, too. 592

The years have had their ups and downs. However, now I know the bad periods will pass. I have actually found that talking about suicide and death helps. I have found it more beneficial to talk about how I feel and why, than attempting it. I felt safe talking to my general practitioner about these issues. He offered a safe environment, his office. I knew that I wouldn't be subjected to unnecessary medication, or detained in hospital. He trusted me and I would not betray his trust. His words were, 'Don't do it again. It is not your time.' It allowed me to be honest. It gave me a chance to grapple with the situation and finally I found self-acceptance and a more positive outlook and reality.

It didn't matter that I was well-educated and more than capable at my job, with a comfortable lifestyle, children and close friends, and an apparently happy marriage. In the past eighteen months, I lost my health, my marriage, my job and my sense of purpose and self-esteem.

If it wasn't for my general practitioner, psychiatrist and counsellors, and the care and support of my family and a few close friends, I might even have lost my life. And it wasn't as if I could do anything about the onset of depression. Unbeknown to me, work colleagues first started noticing my mood swings, increasing pessimism and personality changes more than two years ago. Depression had crept up on me.

By the time my marriage collapsed eighteen months ago, I was on the verge of a massive crash. The marital separation pushed me over the brink into a black despair that I am still fighting.

Grieving and in denial, I became a recluse, a prisoner in my own home. I shunned all social contact and was unable to carry out the simplest of tasks, let alone report for work.

For months I believed there was nothing I could do about my depression. I was so afraid of the shame and judgement of anyone finding out about my inner pain and sadness. I cried. Cried over the unfairness of it all, cried from the aching for happiness that I perceived in the lives of others.

Finally, at the insistence of family and friends, I confided in my general practitioner, who diagnosed clinical depression and prescribed antidepressant medication. Despite being closely watched by him and mental health workers he contacted, I began to behave in an erratic, self-destructive manner, I self-medicated with alcohol, and soon I found myself in trouble with the law for the first time in my life.

My internal voice was all the time telling me over and over how hopeless and pathetic I was. Then came self-harm and suicidal thoughts.

It was weeks before doctors, mental health workers and counsellors could convince me that I needed intensive treatment for my depression in a private mental hospital.

I had to overcome my misplaced pride, and fear of the stigma. I had to make a response when everything seemed out of control but once I did, once I agreed to seek further help, I was on my way to recovery (although I didn't see it that way at the time). It took a long time for me to accept that these people kept encouraging me to seek help not because I was worthless or a failure but because I was suffering from a serious illness and they cared for me.

66

When my depression was at its worst, it was like there were two me's inside my skin—Depressed Me and Real Me. Sometimes

Depressed Me became so big that Real Me became an idea, a memory. And to stay afloat I had to hang onto that idea like a life buoy. The longer I was depressed, the harder it was to stay afloat. Sometimes I wondered if I would ever come back. **579**

Depression is funny in the fact that one day I can feel good and the next day I am unable to get out of bed. I will stay there all day, unable to do the simple things in life that most people take for granted. I will not shower or eat, as it is all just too much for me at that time. Time seems to drag and I have trouble filling my day, even though I may have so many things that need to be done. Destructive thoughts go through my mind and I would wish they would stop, but am unable to stop them. People who have never suffered from depression do not understand how tiring it can be to have your mind going continually and be unable to turn it off. I try to sleep my day away as it is easier to sleep than to put up with what is going through my head.

This is what I find the hardest: the negative self-talk, and the re-runs of events that you would like to change the outcome of, that keep going on and on; the times when all you want to do is to end your life and are so convinced that you would fail at it, because you feel that the rest of your life is a failure, so why would you be able to be successful at this. Sometimes, I just sit and stare at a point and if you asked me what I was looking at, I would be unable to tell you. I have lost hours upon hours by just staring. **520**

I read Marcel Proust and James Joyce instead of my textbooks because I believed that reading about depression could make it romantic and, therefore, a good thing to have. It didn't. Adults would tell me that these were the best years of my life, which only made me want to die quickly because how could I tolerate another sixty or seventy years of this desperation and loneliness? After several suicide attempts didn't work, I found professional help, surely the best move I have ever made. Those doctors saved my life as surely as if they had removed a tumour from my brain.

171

Depression is absolute pain and can be debilitating as paralysis, and, in the blackest moments, suicide can seem easier than enduring the waking hours of the day.

My friend was a casualty in a dark war that millions of people across the world have to fight every hour, a silent battle that takes place in the mind, a battle that is ultimately fought alone and without light. My friend had dug deeply into his mind and, without warning, it collapsed around him. We learnt later that he rang all of his friends before walking into his studio and closing the door behind him. He never mentioned how he felt, only that he wanted to see us soon.

449

For the last fifteen years I have been living with depression, every day, every hour, every minute, every second. It does seem endless. This has been my reality for so long that at times I did not believe that it would ever change, but this way of thinking only ever leads to suicidal thoughts.

So I yell at myself aloud—STOP IT! Then I try to take control, control of the mind within a mind, of thoughts that are just thoughts after all. I must admit that things have only recently improved, but previous to this, when everything went dark, it was the darkest it had ever been and became the blackest years of my life. It was outside my control, as if an alien monster was inside my head trying to destroy not only my mind, but also my ability to live and breathe.

It has been a long, hard struggle on a bridge that kept falling from beneath me, but I am still here, because I realised that I deserve the best life that I can give myself. It is not an easy journey, and I still keep falling, but I want to get up and keep trying, because it does get easier, no matter how dark the path might seem.

Now I try to look at the future as a beginning rather than a dead end. My advice? Seek out help in whatever form you need and keep searching until you find the help that is right for you. Don't be afraid to move on to another form of help when, and if, it seems appropriate—after all, it is *your* mind, body and future at stake.

400

I survived my last bad bout of depression on a diet of lolly snakes and television. Depression won't kill you. You may kill yourself. You could die from an inability to feed yourself but it is unlikely. Don't give up. There is hope. It will pass. The Beast may plague your thoughts and feelings but don't believe or act on them.

91

All is not lost. Don't listen to the songs of the dark sirens—you owe it to yourself not to make the decision when the darkness is all around. Wait until the light comes. Life can be much more than just running from depression—there are many more people like you and me. The hope of a good life glows more and more. Make the effort, even if it's only one of choice.

I choose to beat depression.

Live and live and live until nature, or Fate, decides it's time.

When I'm in the depths of my depression, I wonder if I will ever feel 'normal' again. When I am stable, I fear I will never feel 'real' again.

Depression sucks the life out of you. Your energy, your positive views on the world. When you have depression the world is twenty shades blacker. It becomes so hard to move, let alone be 'normal'. Everything goes so slow and at a thousand miles an hour—and you don't have control of any of it. A corny toilet paper ad makes you cry and the most simple tasks are so hard to do. You can't explain to anyone else how you're feeling because you don't know how to define it. You just call it depression—and hope they understand. Some people will tell you to get over it, but it's never that easy. You feel like there is a box of bricks sitting on your chest and pulling down on your heart.

You can have depression that starts as feeling sorry for a homeless person and it can turn into a month of the blues. You can't pick when it's going to happen or how severe it's going to be.

Ever since I've had depression, I've been trying to escape it.

I've smoked a lot of pot, getting so ripped you can't even feel your face let alone think about how depressed you are. Alcohol, too, drinking myself into oblivion. My every afternoon ritual after school—a bottle of sherry and a packet of smokes with my mate.

My next feat was gambling, starting when I was seventeen. I played the pokies almost every recess, lunch and after school. The club I went to was just across the road from school and they never checked my ID. On my eighteenth birthday I showed them my ID. They were not too happy with me after that. I spent almost every day for the next three years gambling. I say almost, because the clubs were not open on Christmas Day. Trust me, I checked. I sold a lot of my belongings, did countless 12-hour pokie-playing sessions, and lost all of my money and some other people's money. I lived on coffee, cigarettes, beer and poker machines.

My anger was another escape from my mood disorder. I had frequent outbursts at school. No-one gives you an A+ when you're throwing chairs at them.

I'm not trying to glorify or make light of what I have done, because there are a lot of things I shouldn't have done and I feel shame for. It just makes it easier if I put it a bit lighter. **127**

At times I was consumed with a black rage so violent, so appallingly sharp, that I drove my car home like a weapon. **606**

If you are looking for me, you will need your torch and an endless supply of batteries. Don't expect any guidance from me as you descend into the darkness that is my world. Walk through it slowly and take care not to disturb its being. We keep to ourselves—there is less damage that way. **601**

Depression can be short-lived and intensely dark, or it can be a creeper that slowly engulfs your entire being, and, in my experience, totally debilitates you for prolonged periods. Most people would have heard the expression, 'The lights are on but nobody's home'. For me it's more like, 'The lights are out, but I'm home and feeling very alone'. It's a terrifying place to be. You have the key to the room you're in, but are unable to find the keyhole. Mostly you're just unable to look for it.

Sometimes I've gone the wrong way and reached for the booze and drank myself into a much deeper depression. I've become hostile and rejected the help of loved ones. This has proven to be catastrophic for me in the past. My doctor mentioned a logo he'd seen on a T-shirt that really sums me up when I'm going through these episodes: 'Yes, I hear voices in my head, and they don't like you!'

626

There's always a funny side to even the most abysmal situation. Even my suicide attempt failed. I ended up laughing and crying simultaneously at the sheer frustration of not even being capable of killing myself. Another time, after weeks of dilly-dallying, the night had finally arrived when I resolved to go through with it. I decided to watch TV before retiring to bed for the last time. *Coronation Street* was on and it was such a gripping episode that I felt compelled to watch the next exciting instalment. The following day dawned and I'd turned the corner. Life was worth sticking around for after all.

629

One day I woke up. I looked around at the desolation and thought: this can't go on. From that point, I started to fight, to begin the battle—I knew it would be tough, but I persisted and fought for my life.

315

How I hate how much time I've had
to spend on staying sane. I could save
orphans, or learn Sanskrit with all
those hours of crying, gazing and
contemplations.

5. Stepping stones
Diagnosis and disclosure

Being diagnosed . . . shuddering as it was, was also the first step I took towards understanding and attaining some control of my life.

338

Seeking help for the depression that is crushing the life out of your days is a fundamental step to recovery. Ironically, however, the shock of receiving an official diagnosis sometimes leaves people spiralling further out of control. It is not uncommon for people to resist help and continue to deny the intractability of an illness label.

I wept when I was diagnosed and placed on 'chill pills'. I still cannot comprehend that I, the bright, bubbly socialite, have a mental illness. The strong, stable, has-it-all-together go-getter has depression.

376

My diagnosis broke the hearts of all the people around me.

For others, receiving a medical diagnosis is a turning point that brings immediate relief—structuring their experience and providing the chance to access information and develop knowledge to bring order to the chaos that was previously unnamed and unidentified. The ordeal no longer lacks reference points and there is the hope of a pathway out of the darkness.

> I can see now that the diagnosis was the turning point in my life. However, at the time, I thought it was the end of the world.

In this chapter, the focus is on both the distress and the relief of receiving a diagnosis, and what coming to terms with it entails. Once depression is accepted, however, a related problem is raised: *disclosure*. Though clinical depression is an illness, many people feel shame in admitting they have it. Fear of stigma fuels this silence and, as illustrated in this chapter, it can take many years for individuals to feel a sense of pride in surviving the illness, rather than feeling like they have something disreputable, like a character flaw, to hide. Sadly, this reality only serves to compound the loneliness and 'otherness' of depression.

The issue of disclosure also highlights the dangers of denial, especially within families that have a genetic propensity to depression. Some entrants wrote of their distress upon learning of their family's 'little secret'. They felt that more open discussion and admission of the problem with their families could have greatly reduced years of confusion for everyone. Having knowledge of a possible inherited vulnerability might have prevented needless heartache.

In these narratives, writers advise others not to waste time defying a diagnosis and fighting the reality that their behaviour and emotions may be no longer something they can fully control. The sooner the condition is accepted, the sooner steps can be taken along the road to ameliorate such pitfalls.

> I don't feel ashamed and I don't try to hide it anymore.
> I 'came out'.

303

Recovery

I was the eternal domestic,
cheerfully throwing the plates, cups, teapots, everything
out the window, so I'd never have to face washing up again.
I was a wild woman, driven by the moon,
begging the west wind to blow through
and clear all the cobwebs from the house.

Now, I'm a castle in ruins
after years of siege and attack.
I'm the land laid bare
by rising salt and insufficient water.
I'm the shipwreck high and dry
on the sand, rusting quietly away.
I'm a skeleton, stark white,
picked clean by scavengers.
I'm compelled once again
to rewrite my story.

My story is quite a simple one; how the world changed in a day.
One day I was 'normal', next thing I wasn't. I'm no longer in a
position to take things for granted. I can't even count on myself
and my own judgement anymore.

My poem 'Recovery' was written after another bout of mental illness. They call me a manic depressive, a handy label for a cluster of experiences I would rather not have to deal with. It's not that I'm in denial. I make every effort to take control. To do otherwise would condemn me to repetitive cycles of hospitalisation—an experience that I'm not keen to repeat in a hurry. The loss of personal freedom is a bitter pill to swallow, no matter how nutty you might be, or even how much it might be necessary and 'for your own good'. All those people shuffling, shuffling around the locked ward looking for a way out are not tapping into how good it is for them. They are just missing freedom and wanting out.

When I was diagnosed, I was twenty-nine, mother of a five-year-old, working, writing and performing poetry, and highly sociable. It blew my life apart. Reaction to finding out about a mental illness is like any other grieving. Different parts of yourself react differently. Part of me became very stoic. Another part was a blubbering fool. Another part just wanted to make the most of the time I had. What other option is there? Get on with it. You also go through the stages of grieving—of anger, of 'Why me?', of acceptance, of despair. As with any grieving, these stages fluctuate and you swing between them depending on what's happening out there in the world.

While I accept the convenience of a label, and it makes sense to have a shorthand way of conveying a complex cluster of symptoms, it becomes a problem when the label is seen as the extent of the person and the individual differences are not teased out or taken into consideration. We are all many things. I am many things. I am a mother, a handyman, a painter, a gardener, a writer, a musician, amongst other things. While none of these things takes away from the fact that I have a mental illness, having a mental illness also does not take away from these.

When people find out I have a mental illness (and living in a small town makes it hard for them not to know), I am often amazed by their reactions. They say, 'Oh, you're not mad' (well, not all the time!), or 'You can't have manic depression'. Do they think I made it up? Do they say that to a diabetic? From some I get patronising tones. Is it to denote quite firmly that they are different/OK/even better than me, because they don't have a mental illness? Do they think I chose this? Do they see it as a weakness on my part? Do they blame me for having a mental illness? Do they also blame diabetics for being sugar intolerant and having insulin embarrassment? Despite all the best efforts, there is still a long, long way to go before the stigma of mental illness is overcome.

This is not one of those happy endings. It wasn't like going to the doctor thinking I had cancer and finding out it was just a cyst. This is a 'you're stuck with it' situation and I have it for the 'term of my natural' . . . It's impossible to get life insurance. It's pretty tricky to get work. Luckily my son is now grown and I don't have to try and get him to a safe place when I feel myself losing it. I have become reasonably adept at reading the neon signs, the cues that warn me that all is not well. I have methods and strategies in place that keep me on a reasonably even keel. I eat well, I exercise, I only smoke when the pressure gets beyond a certain level. I treat alcohol with respect and I have perfected forms of meditation, one of which includes lots of time in the garden nurturing plants. I have tried working after a stint on the pension. One casual job worked. The other was a disaster.

I don't blame myself for this. I spend a lot of time writing. I have a lot of love in my life—a loving partner, a loving son, loving family and loving friends. I have some friends who are great reality checks for me. When they see things are amiss, they call it like it is. I have had to let go of friends who were aggravations to the spirit. I have a good doctor.

Still I have episodes. The trick for me is trying to minimise their severity, and lessen the time taken in recovery. Keeping things as simple as I can.

It's been twelve years since I was first diagnosed as being clinically depressed and for ten years following that diagnosis I struggled to understand or acknowledge the black dog that had sunk its teeth into me. In fact, I was of the opinion that people, particularly young, fit, red-blooded men, didn't suffer clinical depression in the first place.

Growing up in a Catholic family, I was taught that a man should be stoic, resilient, never show weakness, rarely show emotion, roll with the punches, work hard, marry and support a wife and kids. In my father I recognised all of the above traits and qualities. I wanted to be like him, wanted to make him proud. 'A man's man' was the phrase I hoped others would use when referring to me.

Mental illness was not discussed in those days. Not in my home, at school, with one's peers or in the community. Admitting you had a mental illness like depression just didn't happen. Unfortunately, the terrible stigma attached to having any mental illness was common. In fact, not much has changed to this day. Reactive depression was accepted when a tragedy occurred such as a death or physical illness. But to be depressed for no apparent reason wasn't. I thought it was a cop-out, a sign of weakness, particularly for a man.

Even in my late teens and early twenties, deep in my conscience I had doubts about my character and ability to live up to my own and others' expectations. I had a sense of being a bit different. By that I mean a bit more sensitive than others, a bit thin-skinned, a little more insecure, and a sense that I might not measure up.

By 1993, I was a twenty-six-year-old country boy living with my future wife, expecting our first child and working in a well-paid job. I had it all, yet I was feeling as low as can be. I'd hit a wall. I didn't want to get up each morning, dreaded going to work, wished I could sleep and never wake up. I cried for no reason, felt guilty about my lack of interest, energy and motivation. I felt like a failure and my being on this earth a waste of good oxygen.

I didn't believe the doctor when he said I was depressed. I shuddered at the thought that taking a pill each day would get me back to 'normal'. I thought I must have a virus because 'real men don't get depression'. Only wimps and malingerers got depression. They used it as an excuse for their weakness of character. The doctor prescribed an antidepressant but I refused to take it. I didn't need pills and God forbid that anyone should find out what the doctor diagnosed. I had to just snap out of it. I refused to admit I wasn't coping with everyday life or that I needed help.

And for ten years following that visit to my general practitioner I fought against the idea that I had a legitimate illness and possibly always would. My memories of that mostly miserable decade are incomplete. A carousel of taking pills for a while, then throwing them out when I felt well, only for the grey fog to return. The black dog had a strong grip and wasn't giving an inch. The merry-go-round continued with suicidal thoughts and attempts to harm myself, hospital admissions, changes to my medications and courses of electroconvulsive therapy. I had a string of psychiatric assessments from numerous general practitioners, psychiatrists and nurses. All the while I had a strong belief that I was at fault, that I was weak and hopeless, and that everyone who knew me must think the same.

I became reclusive, anxious and pessimistic. I worried about everything but mostly what others must think of me. I could no longer hold down a job, was granted a disability pension and told I was permanently incapacitated and would most likely never work again.

Anti-anxiety drugs were added to my medications and soon I was popping them like a child would devour a bag of lollies. Life became a blur with each day melting into the next. Whole years went by that I have no memory of. But things were about to change and the black dog I saw as uncontrollable would soon be a little tamer.

My family has a long association with depression. Dark intractable moods, medicinal brandy, tricyclic antidepressants and numerous admissions to hospital 'for a rest' punctuated my grandmother's latter years. My father tamped down his misery with scotch and Wagner, and my mother not only saw the glass as half empty, she also saw cracks, smudges and completely the wrong sort of glass. Dealing with depression by denial was the family business. Black dogs didn't so much run in the family,

they tore through it in packs. As a child, it was incomprehensible to me that no-one else could see them.

I don't need to either disclose that I have bipolar disorder or
hide it, because I don't define myself by having a mental illness.
I am myself—a partner, daughter, sister, friend, carer and
employee. Yes, there is a very real chance that I will have another
episode of depression which will affect my life. And, if that
happens, then it will need to be treated, as it does with anyone
who has a chronic health condition which becomes acute at
times. Life is unpredictable for all of us—the best we can do is
deal with whatever crosses our path as we walk.

I also think that a lot of people with mood disorders struggle
at times with the guilt of things that they have done when unwell,
which may have affected not only their own lives but the lives of
people around them. It is true that actions such as suicide attempts
and addictive behaviours can have a very real effect on the lives
of people who love you; however, it is also true that every person
is imperfect and makes bad decisions, particularly in times of
difficulty. His Holiness, the Dalai Lama, stated:

> If we allow our regret to degenerate into excessive guilt,
> holding onto the memory of our past transgressions with
> continued self-blame and self-hatred, this serves no purpose
> other than to be a relentless source of self-punishment and
> self-induced suffering. (Cutler, 2003, p. 160)

I feel that the best response I can give to my family and friends
who have been hurt by my past actions is to work towards

staying well and living the best life I can, not only for them but for myself. To incessantly apologise and feel guilty would only send me into a self-destructive cycle that would most likely result in me getting depressed again and repeating the same behaviours which hurt them in the first place. As those who have experienced depression know, there is usually no intent to cause harm to others when you're down, just a profound lack of judgement.

For years, I gritted my teeth and struggled on. I'd fought it for so long, seeing acceptance of drugs as a sign of weakness, proud at least of my independent, suffering struggle. I was afraid treatment would diminish what little was left of *me*.

Here's how it is. I don't suffer from bipolar—I am bipolar. Basically, this means that my emotions and Melbourne's weather have a lot in common. Or, to the uninitiated, when I'm fine to high, I feel great, and when I'm low to lower, I often wish there was another way out of this place.

My first episodes began when I was a kid and they haven't stopped. Before I was diagnosed, thanks mainly to the interesting antics I got up to while I was high, I was seen by all those I had damaged as a difficult and destructive wanker. After I was diagnosed, I was reassessed within the blink of an eye and reclassified as a difficult and destructive wanker with a questionable diagnosis. A diagnosis that fixed nothing. Instead, it made matters worse, as now, many of those who felt damaged also experienced a degree of guilt.

Being diagnosed though, shuddering as it was, was also the first step I took towards understanding and attaining some control of my life. No doubt there are people stronger than me, who were and are able to begin their post-diagnosed lives upon the remnants of their pre-diagnosed, but a year after my 'cranium malfunction' had been labelled, I realised that if I was to have any hope of attaining a clean foundation, I would have to leave and start again.

This is not advice. This is just what I did.

Also, since I had no children to support, and with my first marriage lost, there was nothing to hold me.

Now, separated from my past, I began the long process of sifting through its wreckage. I began to find patterns of behaviour, blatantly clear clues, and finally I came to understand some of the craziness.

My brother once told me that he and my sister had taken it for granted that I would kill myself before I was twenty-one. At the time, I thought the same, and yet had no idea why. Now I knew, and this was freedom too.

One of the reasons my high periods always saw me creating one messy situation after another was that I wasn't a bad-looking fella. Not only that, but when high, I was funny, charming and quite often exciting to be around. Magnetic. In these periods, falling in love, spending money I didn't have and gaining employment was easy. A few months later though, once the moods had changed shift, I'd find myself unemployed, heartbroken or both. More often than not I was also in debt and desperate to be alone. This was what I always found odd about the 'black dog' metaphor. A dog craves company, but when I'm down, I don't. Whether I am next to you, in bed with you, even making love to you, I am an island.

These habits of creating emotional catastrophes are common to many bipolar folk. In fact, it is the culminating effect of them, added to the knowledge that you are destined to create more, that becomes too much for many of us. This is why I've always been proud of myself for making it this far.

Alone, and taking enough lithium to power a tourist bus full of digital cameras, I began a second life in Melbourne. This time though, anyone who came into my life was, after a short period of time, informed of my condition.

Two jobs later, both of which I was retrenched from shortly after I'd revealed my secret, taught me that perhaps it was better if not everybody knew. In my private life though, with the medication keeping me fairly stable, I found people weren't that bothered. Most knew someone else who was bipolar (or someone who suffered from depression) and, caught up in their own lives, they left it at that. This was freedom: the freedom of being accepted for who I was and not what I had done.

When I first met my second wife, I informed her, almost immediately, about the other aspects of my head. If she chose to stay, she should know the risks. At first I was fine, so secretly she thought I was exaggerating the problem. If there was a problem. But then I got sick and she changed her mind. Being half-crazy herself, she chose to stay.

After the birth of our first child, our son, I experienced a crisis. I didn't want my boy to grow up with a dad who had to be medicated. Oh my, the stigma of it all. So, with my wife willing to take the chance, I stopped taking my pills and instead tried a healthier diet, plus exercise.

Unfortunately this didn't work. I got sick again. But I am still glad we tried. Hard as this was, knowing where my boundaries lay gave me a sense of freedom too. Freedom from doubt.

Down deep enough to mine for coal, I visited my local general practitioner to get back on lithium. It's a pain in the arse sometimes, but that's the compromise I am willing to make to try to maintain the life we have built and, hopefully, are building. Sadly, in the future, we know that there's a good chance that one of our children may show symptoms. But if and when that occurs, we will deal with it. At least we will know what it is. Then again, who knows what will happen? Maybe even something good. Because, contrary to how you feel when you are down, the odds are always even.

338

I didn't change because I didn't believe there was anything wrong. I denied I had a mood disorder. But if you don't learn from it, it may just be a big black hole in your life. The sooner people start believing they have a mood disorder, the sooner they can be helped.

454

Diagnosis is not an excuse to opt out of life—it's a challenge to get on with it. The aim is to co-exist because you are stuck with depression whether you like it or not. Join the club—you're not alone. At least you know there's a reason for the unrest and mood swings. After the bad news, comes the good—disability can be controlled.

162

It was simply a diagnosis. It means I suffer from a treatable, curable illness. I am no longer the problem, rather, it is this illness that I just happen to be a sufferer of.

447

The most difficult words I have ever had to speak are these: 'I have depression.' In my eyes, these are the most powerful words in the English language. With these three words you can lose friends that you have had for a lifetime, make enemies with people you have never met, and lose opportunities that would have been laid out in front of you had you not had the courage to speak these words. These three words can have you questioning your own sanity, have others question your sanity, and have many assume you are insane. Yes, these are the three most powerful words I know. 'I have depression.' And, for the first time in my life, I am not ashamed. I am not afraid to stand up and let the whole world know.

309

Diagnosis was the moment when my life spun on a coin and could have gone one way or the other.

342

Reflecting on my own journey, I realise that for many years I fought against accepting or dealing with the recurring depressions which are part of having bipolar disorder, and would simply flail around in self-destruction and hopelessness. But I now value these experiences as being a powerful force in shaping who I am today. I have discovered that learning to find meaning in the midst of suffering is a journey in itself.

101

Mental illness was rampant in my family, like a virus that spread. Why didn't they tell me? I could have sought treatment way before my life started to crumble into nothingness. I have lived with the dark clouds every day of my life, believing that there was something wrong with me—if only they had told me, if only they had warned me, if only they had protected me from so much pain.

Depression, because of the lack of understanding around it, can be one of the loneliest diseases. Throughout my journey, I have come across so many people who do not warrant that depression is a medical problem and believe that you can just shake yourself out of it, if you really want to. Again, from experience, I know that this is not true, although I wish it was as easy as that. I have found that with some people it is just easier to pretend that everything is OK; and when I have severe bouts of depression, it has been easier to just pretend I have a virus or cold to stop the inevitable questions that would follow if I told the truth. Any questions are just too hard to cope with when you are not feeling at your best. This is the reason that this disease can be so alienating, isolating us from the people around us.

I have found that some people will accept you and some people will not. I have found that the people who can accept you are great to have around, and usually they are people who have a positive outlook on life. Don't get me wrong, they do not always know what to say or what to do to help you, but they will take you at face value and do their best to minimise your suffering.

'You have depression,' the psychiatrist says, and writes a prescription for a blister pack of antidepressants. 'The depression will pass,' she assures me. 'But you need to see me once a week and take your medication. Can you promise me that?'

'I don't know. I don't think I want to get better. It's too hard.'

She presses her lips together and sighs. 'Then you will have to go to hospital.'

'NO!' I stare at my hands twisting themselves into knots on my knees. 'It's okay. I'll do it.'

I see her once a week for a long time. We argue. She says I am immature, and, to prove it, I sulk. Sometimes we go around and around the same themes for weeks.

'I'm not pointing the finger,' she explains. 'I'm just showing you the toxic patterns set up in your life. I think if we change some of these patterns, you will be a lot happier.'

So:

I get a job.

I take up beading.

I apply for a graduate program at uni.

But the real change begins when I stop pretending.

It starts when I run into an old school friend in the supermarket. I'm in the bread section and, because it's school holidays, the aisles are shrill with sticky seven-year-olds. I've got my head down, cutting through the trolley traffic towards the '12 Items or Less' checkout, when a blonde girl squeals and clutches my elbow.

She pulls off her sunglasses. 'Hi! How are yooouuu?' she asks in that extended manner, which seems to be mandatory when you haven't seen someone in ages.

'Hi Melanie. What are you up to these days?' she asks.

'Oh you know . . . I've just finished my corporate law degree and now I'm just running around getting a few things for a dinner party my partner and I are hosting tonight!' (Said with tight little half-smile.) 'You?'

I scratch my dirty ponytail instead and blurt, 'I have depression, actually, and I haven't been too well'.

'Oh.'

I notice she wears a glittery engagement ring. 'You're engaged. Congratulations.' I wait for her exultant smile.

'Yeah.' She covers the ring with her right hand. 'I'm so sorry to hear you have depression. My fiancé has depression as well. So I sort of know how you must feel. I hope you feel better soon.'

I get into my car with my eyebrows hovering above my head.

But I still feel like my pride is splayed out on a main road, waiting for a road train. I can just imagine what people will be saying about me when the gossip filters back. 'Did you hear about . . . ? She's had a total nervous breakdown and is living at home.' I can imagine my old friends and how smug they must be feeling about their nice boyfriends, sensible car repayments and hire-purchase fridges.

So I avoid them even more.

Then I join a gym and become nodding acquaintances with Grant, whose arms are divorced from his torso by a hedge of muscle and sinew.

'I'm a brickie,' he tells me one day. 'I see you here most days. Where do you work?'

'Well, I have a part-time job waitressing, but I don't work that much because I'm a bit sick. I have depression, you see, and . . .'

There is a funny pause. 'That's no good.' He lowers his head and looks at a spot near my left shoe. 'Nah, yeah. I went through a bit of that meself when I broke up with me missus last year. Had to take six weeks off work to get my head together.'

I go home and call my friends. Friends I haven't spoken to in months. 'I have depression,' I tell them.

Some of them are angry and say things like, 'You're not the only one you know, everyone gets depressed. Just get over it.'

I feel guilty but I also think, 'They wouldn't say this if I told them I had diabetes or a broken leg'. Most of them are sympathetic and gasp, 'Why didn't you say something? We're always here when you need us.'

I start getting text messages from old work colleagues asking me how I am and if there is anything they can do to help. When I check my email now, my in-box is full of e-cards and notes from people telling me how much they miss me. Then a yellow envelope addressed to me in big green loopy handwriting arrives. It's from a man I met only once at a work party. The letter says: 'I am sending you happy vibes.'

I know I'm supposed to feel grateful. But I don't.

I feel proud and exonerated. I don't have to smuggle myself away anymore.

It's been six months now. I still don't have a boyfriend or straight hair or an amazing career as a corporate lawyer. I'm studying to be a teacher and am living in a rented hovel with my brother. But it's good enough.

Twenty-six years have passed since I became ill with a mood disorder. I believe I have successfully managed to recover and build a life of which I can be very proud. I have never shared my story before. It has been a closely guarded part of my life— my own dark night of the soul. For those friends who have stumbled across my vulnerability, I have given brief explanations. We live in a society that still does not look kindly upon those who have suffered in this way.

Take heart. History is full of honourable
people, worthy of great admiration,
who were stark raving mad.

292

6. Finding a way
The power of acceptance and responsibility

> Accept, adapt, monitor—I see it as a journey because I don't think you necessarily find the right match for yourself in terms of medication, therapy, therapists, or approaches overnight.
>
> 110

Acceptance is integral to learning to live with depression. With acceptance comes the possibility of integration, adaptation and accommodation—components that enhance people's ability to effectively monitor and manage the illness.

However, acceptance does not mean that depression is *embraced*, as one entrant sums up:

> Complete and constant acceptance of such a disruptive illness is unrealistic. Acceptance of this part of my life will ebb and flow.
>
> 558

Many people acknowledge their depression as an illness, and continue to see *no* redeeming feature in it at all. This is also acceptance. In such cases, depression is acknowledged as an inescapable reality that individuals simply have to learn, with gritted teeth, to contend with.

Thus, there are different ways to accept and co-exist with depression. Some people maintain an awareness of their vulnerability and are careful to reduce stress in their lives. Some maintain a commitment to regular appointments with their general practitioner, psychiatrist or therapist. Acceptance also acknowledges the possibility of relapse and the need for vigilance, in order to recognise and manage signs and symptoms of an impending episode.

By accepting depression, I no longer dreaded when it was going to appear. Nor did I resent its presence when it did appear. I started being in control and took heed of warning signs.   514

In this chapter, the stories illustrate how people struggle to integrate depression into their lives and their identity, and how acceptance paves the way to more effective day-by-day management.

To live with depression is to understand give and take; that sometimes surrender is the best medicine. As individuals mature with depression, they begin to identify with their illness, and aim no longer at abolishing the disease, but at living with it; at sustaining one's self as meaningfully and healthily as possible.

While coping strategies vary from individual to individual, there are several common threads. Certainly, it is clear that exercise and a healthy lifestyle are essential to living with depression. While connection may seem an impossible task in the depths of a depressive episode, a healthy, supportive social network—a community of sufferers—is essential. Although medication and therapy may not provide a 'cure', they are certainly effective tools in managing depression. Also, engaging and meaningful work can provide the focus and involvement necessary to get through the day, to shift the attention away from one's self.

Living with a severe and debilitating disease such as depression requires relentless efforts at adaptation. There is a fine-tuning of our emotional intelligence that occurs after years of living with depression. Just as a blind person relies on touch and hearing, the depressive uses a heightened sense of feeling to predict how he or she might need to approach a certain day, understanding potential triggers and available techniques to quell symptoms. This accumulated self-knowledge often means less struggle, and provides the courage to have a bad day. To live with depression is to effectively navigate the landscape of your disease. In other words, one must learn to battle the disorder while constructing a life based on its continued presence.

Black dogs are notoriously resistant to obedience training. They skulk around your legs when they should be off fetching; they get in the way and trip you up; they bark so much you can't hear yourself think. Coming when you call is seldom a problem—the typical black dog is rarely far from your side anyway—but try to get one to roll over, play dead or even sit. Such disobedience is endemic across breeds.

My own black dog is a chihuahua, though it started life as a Great Dane. That's one good thing about black dogs. They're no good with children, and they'll never bring your slippers, but they can evolve. Or maybe it's the owner that adjusts, man and beast finding ways to co-exist. Your average black dog will never be a pet, but it can be a companion. Perhaps not one you'd necessarily choose, but one you can abide. I know one man whose Rottweiler became a corgi. Only after a bit of hard work, mind you, and that furry coffee table isn't one Her Majesty would welcome, but nonetheless the cur is now a hell of a lot easier to live with.

The most difficult lesson I've learnt is that there is no point in worrying about what others think or say about you. I've learnt not to feel guilty for having depression. I now know that some people will never be able to accept that the black dog is real and that he can't be driven away easily. I also know that you can only help de-stigmatise mental illness when you yourself believe and accept it for what it is—an illness.

I have depression. I'm not proud of it, I'd much prefer I didn't have it, but I no longer feel the guilt or shame. I can live with that.

105

I am so au fait at living with the black dog that I am over it. For twenty-two years the beast has hounded me, sometimes on a fortnightly basis. I thought she was shaken off for good last year after an eight-month disappearance. Then, blow me down, she pounces again just as I hit my strides last December. She comes crashing at the door, pitching me headlong into despair. *Swallow your words, girlie. Take that: wallop.* It is too easy to be glib and trite. Eat right, sleep enough, exercise, see friends and so forth. Try putting that into practice when the werewolf pins you down by the throat.

I know all the right things to do. Hell, I've had enough therapy and counselling to float an armada of complaints. And, yes, it does help to an extent.

But what works best for me is admitting I have depression, accepting that's where I'm at, knowing it will pass, and riding it through. Usually, there are stressful triggers that spark the affliction and often there is no way to avoid those events in my life. I just try to minimise stress.

Having an understanding family and friends is wonderful, a comfortable bed essential, decent reading material or a few funny DVDs around. Sometimes I am able to knit. Don't expect anything. Do as much as you can and the Schwarzer Hund will (slowly, in my case) remove herself. It may take a week but I can live with that these days. Catch up on rest and repair yourself for what comes next.

91

I personally have reclaimed 'melancholy' over 'depression', as a more delicate, sombre word that better describes my fragile state of mind during episodes of overwhelming sadness when life is a torment, when everything seems to be tinged with grey, when I feel useless and a failure, and wonder why I was ever born.

I am well aware that it is simplistic to suggest that simply changing the name of a condition could possibly improve it in some way. However, for me, knowing that today, and throughout history, many of the world's most accomplished and talented individuals have suffered melancholy helps to remind me that I am in exalted company; that those of us who are doomed to suffer are not condemned or unlucky but, in fact, quite the opposite: we have been given the opportunity, even the privilege, of using our acute state of mind to see through the shallowness and meaninglessness that pervades the lives of so many less-fortunate individuals who cannot accept that we are not meant to be happy all the time, or who fail to realise that success is often empty and always fleeting, and that fulfilment is not to be found in material possessions, in ownership or domination of others, in power or status, or in physical perfection, and that tragedies and death, too, must be embraced—that for some things there are no answers other than faith, endurance or just acceptance.

156

If I were to name one thing that has defined my journey out of the depression maze, it would have to be acceptance—the 'letting go' of my instinctive tendency to resist 'what is'. Resistance and acceptance are opposite sides of the same coin. Resistance is like jumping into a river and trying to hold back the water; acceptance is allowing the water to wash over you and continue its journey.

There is no magic formula; no blueprint or map; the road can be stony and steep, and crowded with setbacks walling in ambush, but the reward of knowing you are living with depression *on your terms rather than the black dog's* constitutes the cornerstone of recovery.

Living with it involves accepting ownership. Clinical depression is a profoundly lonely, disabling and utterly subjective experience. All depressives forge their own chains, and therein lies one of the affliction's most malignant aspects. One size certainly doesn't fit all when it comes to considering how to live with depression. A healing template to fit every sufferer simply isn't available. Just as you somehow found your own way down into this dark labyrinth, you must somehow find your own way out. Of course, loyal friends, loving relatives and professional counsellors can be of great help—sometimes immeasurably so—but the escape plan must come from inside yourself. And although it might sound preposterous to say so (given the incredible pain of clinical depression), you must genuinely *want* to escape.

'I think, therefore I am,' the seventeenth-century philosopher Rene Descartes famously declared in five words. The addition of a single word registers ownership of my black dog: 'I think, therefore I am *depressed*.' My way of thinking is down to personality more than anything else—I've always been inclined to see the glass as half empty rather than half full, and must constantly struggle to escape the grotesque reality of a world perpetually crippled by poverty, bigotry and war.

For me, living with the black dog is a matter of perception rather than chemistry. When the TV newsreader warns me—all too often lately, it seems—that the next story contains images I might find distressing, I can press a button and look elsewhere. Life is not so amenable. The human brain is fearfully complex. However, it now seems clear that the biochemistry of a depressed person's brain is different to that of someone who isn't depressed. But which came first—the altered chemistry or the negative perception of reality?

Therefore, the central thrust of my efforts to live with depression, on my terms, concerns doing whatever I can to work towards a decent, tolerant and more compassionate world.

Fighting depression requires constant surveillance and vigilance. Instead of forging on as if nothing were amiss, next time I will know to back off, slow down and change things.

When I ask myself how I live with depression that has consumed my existence for so long, the answer is, in fact, simple. I live with it because I am alive, and it lives because I am alive.

We—the 'dog' and I—have a strange and yet often amicable symbiosis. I no longer see this experience of myself, of my life, as external to me: it is *of* me. It is me.

To curse this depression is to curse myself. To run and hide from its shadowy presence is to turn away and deny myself. To want to destroy it is, in fact, a wish to no longer exist myself.

I am thirty-four-and-three-quarters. Divorced. Broke. Unemployed. Single. Childless. I was only officially diagnosed with depression four years ago, but, truth be known, this dog has been my faithful companion since I was around eight years of age.

I have benefited from counselling, cognitive based therapy, psychologists, positive thinking and humanist philosophies, and also from medication and a belief in God, and I am currently in psychiatric therapy.

And I hope one day to be well. To replace the familiar presence of anxiety, despair, hopelessness and, even worse, indifference, with other companions of peace, hope and contentment.

But, for now, this is who I am. For I am the black dog. The black dog is me. And I will not hate myself for this, on top of everything else I have rebuked myself for . . . not this too.

I used to be in a hurry to shake it from my back. To demand of myself a 'wellness date'. To long to achieve a medication-free status by this birthday . . . or perhaps the next . . .

But I have stopped setting a deadline for my healing. This journey is my own. The dog and I will continue to walk each day together until the time comes when I can bend down, pat it on the head, thank it for all it has taught me, and then unleash it forever back from whence it came.

So, until then, it's love me, love my dog. Woof.

Seek information. Understanding can only help to avoid the pitfalls of bitterness and resentment that can eventually consume you. It must be accompanied by an acceptance of the human condition.

There is suffering, not just your own, but in everyone. To live with depression, you must come to know it well—seek insight into your own mind. There is a chink in the armour of despair, for nothing in the universe is constant and unchangeable, and depression is no exception.

254

The black dog is a very demanding pet in that it cannot be ignored, cannot be left at boarding kennels and will often need attention at inconvenient times. The beast and I have co-existed for more than forty years. During that time I've known some periods of paralysis whilst arguing with the beast just in order to move. I've also known periods of insight and periods of great joy.

I think that the greatest lesson I learned was that even great pain can be managed. Managing is not the same as control: it is more akin to tacking when sailing in order to maximise the available wind.

I needed to learn to recognise the things that make me feel bad, and then to try to either remove them from my life or to minimise their impact. At the same time, I learned to acknowledge that there are many good things in my life.

Sometimes, in the depths of despair, it is not possible to see the future as being any different. When this happens, it is often easier to remember highlights from the past. In order to do this though, it is necessary to have the list somewhere of what those highlights are. Deep in despair it won't be possible to remember them.

As the list of highlights grows, the strength of the grip of the black dog diminishes. Each small victory becomes a significant milestone in the greater battle.

First you must turn and face it off. You are the *master* and it is the *subject*. Get a really good look at it, and then reach out and collar it. If you feel afraid, so what? Anything that really matters is always a bit scary. When you collar it, you *own* the dog. You formally recognise that *it is not you but it is your responsibility*. It is your job to ensure that your dog is not dangerously aggressive, is fed a healthy diet and exercised. *You* learn to be the master, just as it learns to be trained.

When it comes down to it, there are only two possible solutions to any of life's problems—acceptance or change. If you can't accept a situation, take some action to change it. If you can't change it, accept it. If we believe we can't accept or change a situation, we could try accepting it—*for now*. By at least making a temporary choice, we are avoiding the stress of indecision. Often, if we can't make a decision, we are left in limbo. Our mind dances between one option (acceptance) and another (change), at the same time feeling inadequate because the problem remains unresolved.

It seemed logical to me that making a decision to accept a situation *for now* would help reduce the stress caused by 'not knowing what to do' and the 'fear of making a wrong choice'.

I believe that the decision to postpone decision-making would result in better choices in the longer term. It would allow time for more creative solutions to be explored. Whatever the ultimate result, in the meantime we are exercising control, no longer at the mercy of our thoughts. When I'm depressed, if I think I'm losing control over my own thinking, I feel worse.

Since then, I have applied the principle of 'accept or change' to many issues that have arisen in my work and personal life. For some, I decided to go for *change*—to take some corrective action or to change my attitude. For others, I chose to simply *accept* that some things happen that I am unable to influence.

But for those situations where I was convinced that I could neither accept nor change things—where I felt trapped, blocked or unable to decide—I chose to accept things *for now*. Having this option has helped me realise that I do have control of my thoughts, even when I feel bad. I have learned that accepting a situation *for now* helps lower my stress levels significantly, making it easier to think logically.

For now is not a fixed term—it could be a minute, a day, a month. It's simply a way of moving away from a problem for long enough to regroup, to reassess, to analyse options and solutions, without being overwhelmed by emotion. It's not a cure for depression, but for me it is a very effective tool for levelling my thoughts. And by accepting the existence of depression *for now*, I'm able to develop better, more rational ways of dealing with it.

It has taken me years to reconcile with the black dog. Now I accept him for what he is. Integral, but not the only part of my make-up. It's just a part of me that wants to be understood.

When I was six, my first guitar teacher made me promise to pass on some of his techniques to at least one other person so that his music would travel out of the valley we lived in and continue, 'long after I am gone'.

This story is my music. This is how I overcame. This is how I survived.

Like a miner digging for coal, I worked through the darkness looking for that elusive thing that powered the light inside me, supplied me with energy to get up in the morning, enabled me to concentrate, to laugh, to be interested in something. I fought the black dog, I brawled with it, I wanted to tear it to shreds, but it took to me like an unbeatable rival that no mélange of treatments, therapy or medication could ever exploit or bring down. No amount of reasoning will ever explain the hateful cloud that lurked over me, and no arsenal of words will ever adequately describe how badly I felt.

I became depressed in my early teens and carried its weight into my mid-twenties. I've been told it's genetic. I've been told it has to do with substance abuse. I've been told it's astrological. I've been advised that medication is the only treatment. I've been told not to take medication. It has even been suggested to me that people who suffer depression are mirrors to the world's suffering and that it is a noble thing to be depressed, something to be embraced.

I've been told it's purely chemical. I've tried hypnosis, special diets, vitamin supplements, health retreats, psychiatrists, psychologists, shamans, scream therapy, re-birthing, crystal healing, thought-field therapy, acupuncture, sand play, exercise, paint therapy, volunteer work and antidepressants. I've cried for twelve hours straight and been admitted into a psychiatric ward. I've played classical guitar in fits of rage, run fifteen kilometres on an empty stomach, read the same line in a book over and over for three hours because I couldn't concentrate, and suffered the side-effects of medication. At one point I lost touch with reality and believed that I would suffer forever, and that things would never change.

When I accepted depression lying down, the black dog mauled me in my sleep. And sometimes when I stood up to fight, I was mauled anyway. So often it didn't seem to matter whether I did anything about it or not. But I realised after digging through the darkness for many years that, if there was a way out, it would only be revealed if I kept on digging. I started treating therapies as stepping stones, rather than solutions. I soon accepted the path of depression as part of my journey through life, an element of my growth that governed my experiences. I also learnt to see interactions with people as ongoing exercises in self-discovery.

Some therapies failed me and only some occasionally worked so there was really only ever one decision to keep making: do I keep fighting today or do I let myself be beaten? When bad weather was coming, I could plan for it or let myself be flooded in. So for years I used treatment to project the best outcome in my battle, but only by committing to this path did I come to the realisation that it wasn't the standing up all the time that was unravelling the solutions; the standing up all the time *was* the solution. This became my technique, my dog's Achilles heel. If I noticed the black dog cowering in the corner after exercise, I did more exercise and something extra to make sure he didn't come back that evening. And if he was there in the morning, I put my gloves on and boxed him a little, even when I felt too depressed to get out of bed. And when I noticed the black dog rubbing up against the people I loved, taking things away from me, making me feel guilty, and destroying my social and family life, I continued to war with him and used my grief and anger to fuel my resolve to *always* stand up.

Because I chose to fight depression like a war, I was always looking to share tactics and strategies to give myself the upper hand. Like a guitarist stealing licks from other players, I wanted to be the best at beating depression. But now when someone suffering depression asks me 'What worked best for you?', I don't tell them about my running or the other hundred things I tried. I tell them it was the standing up all the time that worked best, the decision I made every day for ten years to practise, to keep digging through the mine. Will I stand up and make a racket today, or will I retreat and let myself be beaten without throwing any punches? If I was going to unravel the solution, my answer always had to be 'Yes'.

Yes, I will fight today.

Yes, I will fight tomorrow.

Yes, I will fight the next day too.

This was my technique. This was my music. This was what carried me out of my valley, and carries me still.

It is important for people diagnosed with depression to accept that they have a valid medical condition which, although invisible, can be very debilitating. I find that the longer I am in a depressive state before action is taken, the longer the recovery period. If you are at this stage, you will probably need help to take care of yourself due to the fact that you may experience impaired judgement and decision-making, problem-solving and organisational skills. This, joined with confusion and no motivation, is the reason why you act the way you do and don't seem to be doing much about it.

I've lived with depression for years. I have learnt to acknowledge and accept it; learnt how to live with it without encouraging it too much so that it doesn't take over, but not ignoring it either, because if you do, it may bite.

431

Granted, some days it feels like we are doing battle with the hounds from hell or Cujo himself, but hey, you know the saying, 'Keep your friends close and your enemies closer'. Make friends with the black dog. Dogs smell fear and react to it. Run and they will chase you; stand your ground and they back down.

290

With depression, there is good news and bad news. The bad news is that it will recur. The good news is that you are not powerless. Unfortunately, you don't hear the good news until you have gone through the first unhappy round.

377

There are guidelines for depression, but no cure. Nothing's ever gotten over, just gotten used to. I have what I have—yes, it's a disease, but what do you do? It can be handled and dealt with, like many diseases. Some people despise their black dog too much, turn it into an enemy. Mine's not really welcome, but he's not a foe. Just live, go with the flow, accept, befriend your black dog. It's better to be depressed than dead.

562

Recovery has its own rhythm and it's a slow, slow dance. Forward, back, cha cha cha. Back, back, cha cha cha. Side, side, cha cha cha. Forward, back, cha cha cha.

7. Roads to recovery
On seeking professional help

I realised that nobody can get 'out' of depression—you have to work THROUGH it.

I had a long road ahead.

126

Untreated depression creates havoc in people's lives. As we have seen, depression tends to creep up insidiously and then spreads, corroding lives, opportunities and relationships. Yet the decision to seek professional help is not easy. It is difficult to admit that you are not coping with your life. There is trepidation: the fear of being seen as weak, and that you are not capable of managing your own emotions or in control of your mind. It is also very confronting to have to explain your innermost feelings to a stranger, particularly when you might not know the nature of the problem yourself, and thus lack the words to say it.

Really, I am incapable of explaining what this tangible nothingness of complete ruin actually is.

50

I could not understand why I was suffering, or where the
fear and pain had come from. It was all so alien to me. I was
isolated, not only physically but mentally. I completely lost
the ability to connect on any level with any other human
being. It was impossible to express what I was feeling, as
I had no understanding of it at all.

385

Valuable time is thus lost between symptom onset and
seeking help. This reluctance and hesitation can sometimes
last for decades. It is these periods of unnecessary anguish
that our writers hoped their stories could prevent.

I was my own worst enemy. It was a year before I could
swallow my pride. After two years of depression and
pathological pig-headedness, I went for advice.

522

They implored people to seek assistance early and to not
waste valuable time feeling ashamed, to reach out and grasp
the hands eager to help. 'Do not go it alone,' they collectively say. For most, professional help is a vital link in the
chain of recovery, and it provides a much-needed anchor
and sense of stability—especially early on in the illness.

The difficult part is to take that first step.

170

The idea of spilling my guts to a complete stranger left me
cold. But we talked and talked. I think this is what unleashed
me from my black dog.

529

Although early intervention and treatment are vital steps in the management of depression, recovery often feels like 'one step forward, two steps back'. The journey is not an easy one for, in truth, it is often difficult to find mental health professionals that you 'click with' straightaway. It is hard to come by good recommendations, and then there are the waiting lists and, often, expensive fees.

Seeking help is hard. I found a number of professionals could not empathise with or assist me.

361

During my 'black period' I had a psychologist (who will remain nameless) actually tell me I was a hopeless case. The thought of that statement years ago still riles me. However, maybe he unknowingly lit the fire that resulted in my eventual recovery.

201

The use of medication in the treatment of depression proved to be a contentious issue for many. Some writers were aggravated by the troubling side-effects they experienced in finding a treatment that worked for them. For many, this was a lengthy and frustrating process of trial and error. Others feared possible dependence on their medication and felt uncomfortable with the idea of a synthetic solution—an 'emotional anaesthetic'—to heal their uniquely personal torment.

Life on medication was a continual diet of plain custard. There was no happy, no sad, no desire—all things felt flat and stale.

151

The first choice I had to make involved using a medication to correct the chemical imbalance in my brain. I was terrified. The prospect of lifelong drug dependence hung over me like a dark spectre. I took the first step out of desperation, rather than courage, and was pleasantly surprised.

223

Undeniably, the role of pharmacology in the management of depression is a complex issue, but it is one that must be addressed. Within psychiatry, there is a widely held view that, for certain types of depression—mainly melancholia and bipolar depression—drugs and clinical intervention can be paramount in ensuring functional recovery. Other therapies are of benefit alongside the improved mood promoted by such medication support. For non-melancholic depression, medication is sometimes, but not always, necessary; other treatment options—cognitive, behavioural and social changes—can more readily achieve results. When the right combination is achieved, the effect on most people's lives is profound, and recovery becomes a tangible goal.

The vignettes in this chapter are of individuals' experiences—both good and bad—of medication and hospitalisation, the benefits of counselling, and the necessity for trust, empathy and good communication between clinician and patient to establish a successful therapeutic alliance.

Overwhelmingly, the writers advised patience and persistence.

Contrary to expectation, giving in turned out to be a new beginning.

Being told that the condition will get better is helpful. Be prepared for the long haul. Think in terms of months, and maybe years. This is not something a magic pill can cure.

Depression isn't the kind of illness that you wake up one morning and suddenly have. The same can be said about overcoming depression. In the beginning I was naïve, believing that depression was curable, that I would wake up one morning and it would be gone. But I know now that this is never going to be the case.

To overcome depression requires strength, persistence and a lot of hard work. And sometimes, even when you try your hardest, it just doesn't seem to be good enough. The key to winning the battle with depression is to never give up, no matter how dark, how hopeless, how difficult things seem.

I have recognised that it is up to me to control my depression. It can seem so easy to just sit back, let the world fall down around you, and then blame your depression. I know just how hard it can be to think of the future, of tomorrow, of a life without the pain and suffering associated with depression. But I also know what it is like to overcome depression, and how much there is to live for in this world.

I believe that depression needs to be treated with medication and/or counselling, and that I am the only one with the power to ensure that I persist with this treatment. I take my antidepressants daily, see my psychologist weekly and go to a psychiatrist every few months. For the first time in more than four years, I feel like I might actually have a future. I know that depression will not magically disappear. I have learnt that the hard way. But acknowledging this and knowing that treatment is possible are the first steps to managing and overcoming this illness.

One of the most beneficial factors was accepting that I have a mental illness and that, whilst it cannot be cured, it can be controlled through a good medication regime and regular monitoring. Sometimes it can take months, up to a year, to find the medication/s that best suit you. Everyone is different and therefore a medication that may work great for a friend does nothing for you.

Don't expect the doctor to do all the work and remember they don't have a crystal ball. If you are not open and honest about what you are experiencing, then you cannot expect to get the best treatment plan. If you keep changing your medication dose, or stop taking it without first consulting your doctor, you cannot expect to recover as quickly.

Even when you feel better, you need to continue taking your medication. So many people make the mistake of stopping or reducing the medication, then wonder why they slip straight back into a depression.

The most important resource I have to keep my demons ensconced in their own nightmare, instead of endlessly slithering their way through mine, is my psychiatrist. As I suffocate in the misery of the worst depressive phase I have experienced, one professional extended a hand and offered me reasons to believe I was worth saving. He tells me I have value, that I'm special. Amid my constant turmoil, he is a stable, understanding lifeline and, right now, I owe him my days.

Living with an undiagnosed illness for more than twenty years has required ingenuity and a sturdy catalogue of survival skills, each adapted and perfected through constant use. My ability to ride the highs and lows of bipolar disorder with no support and no real personal understanding of my circumstances was, I see now, quite extraordinary. I created a successful life, littered with wonderful achievements, being highly respected in my professional career and admired for my creative, interesting lifestyle. No-one saw the extremes. I was much too adept at self control, perfectly constructed plans and complete withdrawal, as required.

Crashing through highs and then hurtling down endless, empty chasms was my normal reality and I morphed into whoever I needed to be, so that I could live as well as I imagined was possible. The fantastic phases of activity held special places within, while the deep, dark depths were there only to be endured, perhaps as punishment for my more voracious days. As the gaps between became smaller, my world took on a faster pace and I was scrambling to achieve all I could in the perceived time allotted. My strength began to wane as the pressure increased and, somehow, I lost control of one day, then one week. Isolating myself became an important necessity because there was no energy for anyone else in that mountain of grief that became each day I dreaded facing. The world was a place I didn't know how to be in.

When the pieces of me broke, I had no idea where or how to start looking for them. Every crack I had carefully repaired over the years shattered right at my feet. Every survival tactic I had employed vanished. My soul was frozen—there was no creating any kind of bloom to present to the world. Simply breathing seemed like a new skill to master and I was bewildered by the notion. This was not a battle to keep depression at bay. I needed something much, much more because I knew that I was way out of my depth. The unrelenting pressure of searching for answers, for any solutions to help me live, was intensely distressing. I always believed that I was prepared for anything, but I was frighteningly wrong.

With desperate, tortured thoughts that were laced with clouded memories of instinctual survival skills, I asked for help. It seemed a weak moment for me, so that even with a solution presented, I became immediately dismissive. 'Just talk to me,' I begged my trusted general practitioner, through relentless tears— and then came the quiet confession, finally, of my family's long history of mental illness, the one we didn't speak about. 'You need more than I can give you,' my GP said. 'I want you to see a psychiatrist.' *I am not like my father.* The inside of me was wrenching, further damaging my already fractured soul. Suicide, or an appointment with a psychiatrist? My options felt strangled.

With the fear of every detail of my days, I spent an 'alone period' contemplating how my life had come to this stage. I felt strong convictions that I had cultivated and nurtured every possible means of coping with and managing who I thought I was. A psychiatrist seemed an obscene admission of a life poorly lived and one in complete turmoil. I resorted to denial, then frustration and anger. I became smug, and then determined to just try harder. But I still couldn't breathe right. So I kept that first appointment.

Because I felt as though I had been in control my whole life, there was a dreadful resignation about seeing a psychiatrist. I did have some small spark of hope, but basically I *made* myself ambivalent. How could I describe myself to a stranger, no matter how professional or experienced he was, when I didn't understand myself? Would I have felt differently if I was seeing an oncologist? I'm certain I would have. I didn't know what I should expect from this visit with a psychiatrist. I didn't know what to expect from myself, how I should act, or be. I didn't know what I needed from him, or even if I wanted whatever he had to offer.

After that initial appointment, the details of which remain quite elusive, I threw myself back into everything that was once familiar to me. I did all I was supposed to. I saw friends, answered the phone every time, said yes whenever I was invited somewhere. I eased up on the alcohol, ate healthier, walked every other day, made myself 'think happy'. Any small routine to feel safe and controlled. All the time, I had a small piece of paper with possible explanations of what might be the cause of my severe disdain for life. I tried to toss out that note and each time, I decided to just hang on, to wait and see. Bipolar disorder was not something that could slip by me, but I can't describe how hard I tried to ignore it. I magically decided that the psychiatrist was wrong, inexperienced and clueless.

Before my next appointment, I researched and educated myself on this business of mental illness. I absorbed every word, dismissed every obvious sign that screamed at me. *I am not who my father was.* I am too in control, too successful, too everything, to have a mental illness. Bipolar, anxiety, depression, *lithium* . . . they are not who I am. Still, the deep pain and turmoil persisted and I felt the burden of my life envelop me. I was desperate for answers, desperate for meaning and desperate to reconnect with the psychiatrist. Just in case. I needed someone who I never imagined would be my rock, someone to stabilise my life and give it meaning.

Living with a mental illness takes every ounce of strength I never knew I possessed. The confusion, frustration and desperation of my days mean that I have precious little left to explain the complexities to someone who is healthy. The process is draining, distressing and disheartening. My friends can't understand how or why I am suicidal, and they feel powerless to help. My friends can't see the demons, can't feel the pain, and don't know how my thoughts can be so twisted and frightening. They simply don't know how to manage the me they thought they knew. My psychiatrist won't tell me to 'just think happy' or 'you'll feel better tomorrow' because he knows that I need something more than that.

My psychiatrist knows that when I tumble into 'my sane logical reality', he has to help me sort my thoughts and keep me away from my treacherous danger zone. He is my safety net, even when I don't realise I need one. It's his job to take on the burden of helping me get well. It's a burden I can't allow my friends to assume. I need a professional who knows how I am, and what I need to live well. I need to be able to cry, scream, show anger, feel guilt or misery. I need to be able to explain where I'm at, talk through my fears, celebrate small achievements, acknowledge my failings. I need to feel no pressure to be the perfect someone I was for others, because I am not. I need to understand my illness, argue my perceptions, and express my thoughts without fear of reprisals. I need medications monitored, my compliance in taking them to be worthwhile, and my constant suspicions allayed. The people who love me aren't qualified to be all of this for me. Their instinct is to want to 'fix me' and I despair when they think they have nothing to offer me. They don't see that our bond might crumble if I depend on them, as I do my psychiatrist. I feed on their love to help me live with this illness, but it's my psychiatrist who provides me with what I *need* to live productively, happily even.

To live with depression, you do what you have to. Sometimes, it's just enough to survive through one more day. When my entrenched survival skills deserted me, I called in an expert. I know that he is there when I need a steady hand. He is the commitment I make to myself to get well and I know that I deserve that solid, uncompromising belief from him—that I am special enough.

I expect my soul would forever be vacant if I depended on those who love me in the same way I depend on him. 261

The ache has gone. Long gone. I can study. I can read. I can cook a meal. I can apply make-up and dry my hair. I go out almost every weekend. I even have a boyfriend.

But the ache hasn't been replaced. It's now a nothing.

I am angry with the war in Iraq. Furious at the politicians. I rant and rave with the best of them.

Anyone would be fooled.

Inside I am starting to wonder where I have gone. I'm showing all the emotions, acting them out. But the sweetness that stings in your chest when you really cry is missing. The bubbles that rise from your belly when you really laugh. The fibrillation in your stomach when you really look right into your lover's eyes. All of it—missing. I'm not feeling. Anything. My mind's blank. What's wrong with me?

18

After eight hospitalisations, thirty treatments of ECT, trial and error games with medication, three overdoses and various encounters with psychiatrists, some helpful, some damaging, I became strong enough to begin rebuilding my life and repairing my broken soul.

My admissions to hospital have attached to them an ironic sense of freedom. Sure, I was in a place where my physical freedom was restricted; strict rules dictated the routines of my day. But my unsafe emotions and distorted thoughts were in a space of shelter and rest. No longer having to live a façade granted me a most welcome sense of liberty. I didn't have to pretend that I was coping with such a ferocious illness. Hospital permitted calm and respite when I needed it desperately.

I feel a deep sense of gratitude to the remarkable people I came to know during my stays in hospital. As I listened to their stories, as I listened to their tales of both trauma and incredible courage, I realised I was not alone. We all shared such similar experiences: the literal heartbreak of illness, the frequent interruption of our lives by a force stronger than us, the breakdown of relationships, work and study. Our collective strength formed an extraordinarily tight bond between us all. It was these things we had in common, these familiar journeys of darkness and redemption that developed and sustained solid friendships of trust and admiration.

Depression, especially untreated depression, is dangerous and destructive. Psychiatric medication is a controversial matter but I believe in its benefits entirely. Whilst working closely with many different psychiatrists, I tried many different medications. Some inflated my weight, some caused my body to shake involuntarily. These side-effects were awful and seemed only to add to my misery, but I'd take a membership at Weight Watchers over a lifetime membership at a psychiatric clinic any day. At times I rebelled against taking medication daily, resenting the constant reminder that I had an illness that would stalk me forever. But I eventually came around when I realised that this medication was allowing my mind to reach its full potential. My mind is everything to me, essential to my happiness and sense of self-worth. My greatest fear was that it would not work as it should again, that it would be forever foggy and sluggish, only capable of digesting trashy magazines. But it is not. I am now studying and thrive off my mind's lively, insistent need for thought and reflection.

558

I was piling on the weight with tricyclic antidepressants, but I promised myself I'd worry about that later. I'd take fat and happy over thin and depressed any day.

579

I didn't want to go on antidepressants. Depression is a mental state—if you can't control your mind, what can you control? Who are you? More than anything I wanted to be able to rewire my own brain, teach myself new ways of thinking, shear off my synapses and join them to others, create new paths. If I couldn't do that, then that meant my brain was wired up wrong altogether, didn't it?

'Besides, antidepressants have side-effects,' I said to my frustrated psychiatrist, who replied, 'What's worse—the side-effects of the antidepressants, or the side-effects of depression?'

Good point. Actually the side-effects of the antidepressants made me wonder which really was worse. I was on Prozac when it first hit the market and people were claiming it could cure wooden legs. Prozac woke me up every night, screaming, my T-shirt dripping with freezing water that had come from my very own pores. Some antidepressants made me shake, some made me vomit, some kept me awake all night, some made me sleep all day. One sent buzzing flashes of colour in front of my eyes and one made me lose my sex drive completely. (I decided that was a side-effect marginally less acceptable than the urge to kill myself.) After a year of this—a year—I found one that made my mouth dry, which meant my teeth would be prone to cavities, but I voted to let my teeth take their chances.

Antidepressants don't cure depression, they just take the edge off, give you a fighting chance. At first it was strange. I'd become so used to being felled by a depressive bout every fortnight that when three weeks went by without one, I found myself looking nervously over my shoulder. When would it come? It came a few days later, but was perceptibly less intense. Antidepressants allowed me to do battle with my black dog on a more equal footing.

If there was a literal vicious dog on the loose that was threatening your safety or the safety of others, then it would make sense to call in the professional dog catchers who are trained to deal with this kind of situation and are adequately equipped to do so. Likewise, when that black dog is on the loose and you can't fend him off alone, there is no shame in calling in the professionals. There are many wonderful organisations and people who are willing to offer assistance, a listening ear, a hand to hold, or a shoulder to cry on. Many who volunteer their time, energy and resources are sufferers themselves, past or present. They are well-equipped to help you with that troublesome and menacing black dog. There are medicines available to ease the pain of the nastiest bite. And there is no shame in availing yourself of these if your doctor prescribes them for you. You can't always say goodbye to the black dog, but you can muzzle that mutt and put it to bed.

290

Medication was absolutely necessary for me at first, when I could not draw myself out of the sea of sadness in which I had habitually floated for perhaps two years or more. After three weeks on medication, someone said something funny and I laughed. It was the first laugh I hadn't faked in a very long time. That was a turning point. Things looked up. My focus turned from inside to outside of me, and I gradually reached out to others and got involved in life.

419

Don't go it alone. Most people won't have a clue what you're going through and the more you try to explain it to them, the less they will understand. Accept this and be thankful that they don't suffer. There are plenty out there who will understand

and, in the course of seeking help, you will find them. Get help from as many different sources as you can: books, doctors, websites, counsellors, psychologists, nutritionists, poetry. It may be called depression but it is actually a many-headed monster and must be fought on a number of fronts.

Part of your problem must be seen as a medical condition. See a doctor, but only you can decide if you want to take antidepressant medication. If you do, never rely on medication alone. If you want to reduce the problem down to a chemical imbalance in your brain, then don't forget that your brain chemistry is influenced by the way you think. In fact, your brain chemistry is influenced by what you hear, smell and even say. You brain chemistry is influenced by what you do, and it is certainly influenced by what you eat and drink. These many fronts are too much for one person to handle on their own.

292

I have come to realise that living with the black dog is like living with a dog that is savage, aggressive and unrelenting, but has been chained, bolted and muzzled. That chain has links, and each link has a name—diagnosis, medications, counselling, taking care of myself, adequate sleep and family harmony. As with any chain, it is only as strong as the links are, so if any of my links become weak (if I don't take my medication regularly, or I don't get enough sleep, or I don't go over the strategies learnt in counselling, or there are really big family problems), then the chain holding back the dog becomes weaker and weaker, and eventually it breaks and I am overcome by depression again.

This chain has to be bolted on to something solid so that the dog cannot get loose. That something solid is my self-worth—'I AM good enough', 'I AM worth the effort of recovering'. This bolt is the most important piece of equipment, as without the bolt holding the chain in place, the dog is let loose.

The muzzle on the dog is acceptance of my life as it is—acceptance of myself as I am, acceptance of the dog in my life, acceptance of past painful events. If I take off that muzzle (if I start feeling sorry for myself because of how my life has turned out, or criticise myself for faults that no-one else sees, or look at the damage past painful events have caused), the dog can bark at me about these things.

Even though the black dog has been silenced by being bolted, chained and muzzled, it will still rear its ugly head and, unless the bolt, chain and muzzle are in good order, I will come under its influence again.

Thankfully, I have had the support of loving family and friends, professional psychiatrists and counsellors, who have all helped me enormously in my efforts to maintain this bolt, chain and muzzle. Without their ongoing help, love and support, I would not be able to contain this beast that lives within me. Thank you to them all.

Having been on a plethora of medications over the years and still being on some today, I've come to accept that medications can help with some aspects of depression. However I also believe that we are interconnected in mind, heart, spirit and body, therefore our response to depression needs to acknowledge all these aspects of ourselves. Taking medication can be one of the easiest parts of responding to depression—most of the hard work comes when we ask ourselves how we as a whole person have come to find ourselves in a place where we feel so lost and hopeless, and then having the courage to look for the answers.

At times during admission I became catatonic, unable to move properly and certainly unable to talk. The absolute terror that takes over in such a state is impossible to convey to those not personally acquainted with it. It became difficult to move and my thoughts went into overdrive. My head was racing, and I was beginning to hear arguments raging in my head. In the following weeks I was given massive doses of tranquillisers, and was seen by many doctors. All were concerned. They called it psychotic depression.

I was helpless, I was dependent on the nurses, doctors and my parents for everything. My parents visited every day, as they would on all future admissions. It was heartbreaking for them to see their son like this and it took all their courage to support me. Without their devotion, I don't know if I would have made it.

Slowly, I began to recover. The medication helped, but I also began therapies: I remember my first cognitive behavioural therapy group, learning techniques to turn my tortured thinking around. More importantly I began to talk about feelings, about my beliefs, and found acceptance of them. It was liberating; as a fourteen-year-old boy such things weren't generally discussed.

But it was only the beginning. Over the next three years I was in and out of hospital. The doctors, nurses and psychologists did everything they could. All sorts of medication, and therapies such as art therapy and talking therapies. They all had their place in getting me through, but it was the personal support offered by my family and the staff at the hospital that probably helped the most. I was too unwell to care for myself. I saw no future, but thankfully others did.

418

Psychiatric wards were my main coping mechanism for managing my suicidal thoughts and tendencies, and feelings of utter terror and torment. They were the only places I felt 'understood' and where I knew I could not harm myself. My stays in hospital also gave those who were endeavouring to care for me some breathing space.

322

After several fruitless encounters with my GP, I reached my own diagnosis. Around four long months later, I went to a different GP and got a referral to a psychiatrist. I can remember sitting in the psychiatrist's waiting room thinking my life could never get any lower than this moment. It was the ultimate confirmation that I was completely stuffed, beyond help, never to be myself again.

I was really lucky that she and I clicked straightaway. I trusted her and then I trusted her decisions. She recommended medication. I stalled, finally agreeing. She knew when to take charge and when to let me find my own way through.

I had changed jobs. Nobody tells you that you make really bad decisions when you're depressed. I had a sick day at my doctor's suggestion. When pushed, I told my boss I was a bit depressed. The following day a letter arrived at my front door via courier. I was fired for having depression in a senior job. I can't even describe my mood after this. I dropped like a stone.

Seeing my general practitioner was an anchor in an otherwise directionless week. I read up on depression, every book I could get my hands on. Reading them passed the time, and each one added little bits to my pool of knowledge. Helen Razer's quirky *Gas Smells Awful* about her own experience with depression seemed to help the most. She was writing from inside the Perspex™ box, and it made me feel less alone.

I found that when I cracked the sleeping problems I managed better. My chiropractor really helped and she started acupuncture on me, which was almost miraculous in how it helped my sleep and general energy. Yoga gave depression another good shake-up, and I found it corrected the problem of feeling like my skin didn't fit. It helped my agitation and my worry levels. I went three times a week and this gave my life more structure. The road to healing was really slow, but it helped when I stopped setting deadlines.

Some days were hell. Sometimes the drugs were hell. I changed medication three times. My doctor told me, 'If you can't face the whole day, think about the next hour. If an hour is too much, take it one minute at a time. If a minute is too much, think about your next breath. Say to yourself, "This too will pass".' I killed a lot of days thinking about my next breath. A statement on the internet stuck in my head: 'Suicide is a permanent solution to a temporary problem.'

When I felt a bit stronger, I took my former employer to the antidiscrimination court. It was incredibly hard to face them, but it was an important win for me. Depressed people have rights too! The money I received was a great help in my 'being nice to me' campaign. It allowed me to move into a shared house, do some short courses at community college, and take up horse riding. It's quite easy to forget you're depressed when you're cantering around the countryside. I had glimpses of being happy to be alive.

I began to enjoy recovery. It was a *slow* unfolding of limbs after a long sleep. Things have a serene rhythm. Life has been forced to simplify. Relationships have evaporated or been distilled down to a genuine essence. I created the silence in which to hear my own voice, to hear what I wanted to do next.

I accept that I might be followed around by this black dog forever, that the dog might change size and become ferocious again at some point in the future. That's OK. I hope I will catch it earlier and be nicer to myself the next time, and that this will aid a quicker recovery.

Sometimes it can be the most ferocious beast a person will ever face, and sometimes it's just a small black dog. But if you find one following you or someone you know, don't be afraid. Talk to someone and get help. The real you is still in there somewhere.

579

I am gradually teaching the black dog how to 'sit' and 'stay', and thus learning to manage it. I hope by sharing what I've learnt that others may find their own ways of living with depression. Antidepressant medication helped me sleep better but soon after seeing my general practitioner, we both realised I needed to 'talk' also. I needed to offload, reflect and feel supported.

I needed to develop some strategies, to get out, and stay out, of this blackness. I started seeing a clinical psychologist.

During the first eighteen months after I was first diagnosed, the changes in me were gradual. I felt I was taking one step forward and two steps back. Even minute stressors that came my way would knock me off balance, and it was at these times that the supports around me were so vital.

The dog started to change colour, to 'pastel', as I learnt coping strategies. Occasionally, though, the dog still turns on me, and those teeth can bite! I experience 'swirling blackness' at these times. But because I'm better equipped, these periods are becoming less frequent, less intense, and usually don't last as long.

My strategies have been numerous, and I feel I will continue to learn and add to these throughout my life's journey. I know I will still have 'black' times, but I feel more able to get through them now. Two of the strategies that have worked for me are:

- 🐾 Commencing medication, and then sticking with it (even through the side-effects), until I found the right antidepressant for me.
- 🐾 Regular psychology and general practitioner appointments, tailored to my needs at the time. My general practitioner and I now mutually decide on my medication dose. I feel I have a say in the process.

Both my clinical psychologist and general practitioner are people I feel comfortable with. I was gradually able to become more open with them, and felt they respected where I was at throughout my illness. I appreciate the fact that early on they pushed me only gently. I always felt I was being consulted.

58

By the time I seek help, it is necessary to be admitted to a clinic far from our country property. It is a long trip to Sydney, with neither of us saying much; my husband in shock that I need treatment, and me—well, I'm not in the mood for saying much.

The clinic is frightening in the beginning—it's unfamiliar. I tell my story three times in two hours. There are many people there also suffering from depression as well as those with other problems. After the first few days, when I find it too emotionally tiring to talk to anyone, I find it a relief to be around people suffering like me—people who understand what it is like to feel fenced off from the world. It is also frightening when many of them reveal that this is not their first time here; some have been here several times. I hope that this will not happen to me.

The clinic feels like a sanctuary, a refuge where I can escape from all my worries. All too soon, however, I realise that the black dog has accompanied me and is lurking in my mind, waiting to haunt my sleep. I need to exorcise him—somehow. The medications help, but slowly, so slowly.

Art therapy is offered at the clinic and, for the first time, I work with clay. I love it. Through this medium I seem to be able to work through my emptiness and fill my mind with what I am making, and my hands are grounded by the feel of the clay. I make little figures—sometimes they make me cry but it is meaningful emotion not empty and exhausting.

Meditation and relaxation are also very rewarding. I find it difficult to relax at first but, when I achieve it and can meditate back in my room, it makes such a difference to my ability to sleep and when I become tense in the daytime. Above all, it gives me a sense of control over something in my environment.

We go down to the beach in the bus once a week and although it is in the morning and I am not a morning person, the sense of peace I get from walking along the beach makes it worth the early rising. In fact, simply walking around the block, stopping to look at the view and noticing the gardens along the way, also soothes my soul.

A concept that one of the therapists talks about is 'mindfulness'—the practice of being solely involved in whatever one is doing and not thinking about other things until one has finished. I realise that I have been doing the opposite all my life and resolve to change that particular mind habit. It makes sense that if you concentrate completely on what you are doing, there is no room for negativity feeding depression.

Tai chi and yoga are two more activities requiring mindfulness and although I am a middle-aged, overweight, unathletic person, I find that I can do these activities and they also help to keep depression away. I buy a tai chi DVD, a couple of kilos of clay, and start planning what new plants I need in the front garden. My tiny room soon becomes festooned with cards from friends at home—perhaps I am not as unlovable as I think!

In the clinic I really value the support of other patients. We are like soldiers, engaged in a war against the conditions that affect our minds. There is so much support, so much understanding and so much caring that it makes me feel that maybe I am worthwhile. When we are in groups together, it helps to hear how others are coping with particular issues and to get and give feedback and encouragement; but often just going for a walk with someone and talking about something else altogether will lighten both our moods. Reading also helps. I read for escape but also to gain insight into my depression.

But while these activities are all very well, they are still a means to distract myself from the real issues—my feelings of uncertainty about myself and my essential worth. As I have done all my life, I am relying on what I do instead of who I am. It is as if the essential me is so terrible, so unworthy, that I have to run from it without looking back or instead fashion a mask to hide myself from the world.

After eight weeks I am ready to leave—or so I think! I get home and the rooms are full of flowers from my friends and family and the house sparkles. The next morning I wake up and the roses have all come out in bloom, and the paddocks are green and verdant—so different from when I left. But depression does not respect green paddocks or stunning roses. Two weeks later I am on my way to the psychiatric hospital in the nearest large town. This is mainly due to the shortage of mental health practitioners in rural areas. The only way I can get help is to be admitted to the hospital.

I stay there for two weeks, partly to fine-tune my medication, but mainly to work each day with a psychologist. We turn me inside out, but, in the process, I gain more understanding about the influence my personal history has on my life view and, more importantly, how I do not have to be locked into my vision of myself by what has happened in the past, and I can make a success of living in the future.

Once again I head for home. This time the grass has turned to gold and the crops are ripe and ready for harvest; they look dry and dead but are full of goodness. I feel a sense of peace as I come up the long and winding driveway.

This is who I am, this is where I live—and I'm OK. It is not the end of the battle against depression, but at least I am armed and ready for it this time—and hopefully for the next. 🐾478

Medication helped quite miraculously. I was jubilant. I had found the solution, or so I thought. Medication has almost always alleviated my depression, sooner or later, except for one instance when I needed ECT—electroconvulsive therapy. The social stigma, the subsequent shame at my disorder and the difficulty with side-effects made me stop taking medication for long periods at a time. 'I was a born again normal', until it returned with a vengeance. I think it's called 'kindling': untreated attacks became worse and longer in duration. Now I meekly accept medication and don't try to do without it.

But medication is not the entire answer. I had to learn how to make myself less susceptible to depression, to understand what makes me vulnerable and what helps me cope.

Psychotherapy was important. I learned how to cope better and how to challenge some of my depressive obsessions. Unfortunately, my depression often starts with somatic symptoms, flu-like malaise, bodily pain, lethargy and an awful body image.

After years of psychiatric help, my medication and health are now monitored by a general practitioner with depth of knowledge and counselling skills. The GP will refer me to a psychiatrist should it be necessary. I watch myself carefully for signs of the beginning of an episode and, together with help from my general practitioner, mostly curtail it.

Watching myself like this is tiresome, but it's necessary to get oneself sorted. Some general practitioners (fewer now) who lack knowledge think you are a hypochondriac or even a malingerer, so I'm careful whom I choose.

303

The help I received in hospital was all about learning to live for myself. It may sound selfish, but for me it was all about survival. These are lessons I think everyone should learn— about healthy boundaries, about self-esteem, and about not being responsible for others' feelings. Cognitive behavioural therapy also helped me challenge all my fears of not sleeping, and my insomnia was cured as if by magic. The people I met there were an inspiration to me and I owe them my life.

In the time since I left hospital, I have lived with depression by looking after myself. I see a therapist and also go to a support group. My therapist shows me that I am OK as I am. She helps me, guides me, encourages me and never judges me.

My support group has been one of the most fascinating experiences of my life. It is my safety net, and a place to share the pain and joy with others who have experienced depression. I think we are the healthiest bunch of people I know. Some of us use 12-step programs, some believe in our gods or goddesses, and we all take it one day at a time. We learn from each other's successes and failures, and from the feedback and support we get. I have even discovered my own spirituality— something I never imagined would happen to a cynical atheist like me.

I also have my own private checklist for knowing whether I'm getting depressed again:

1. Do I wish I was dead? (That's a pretty important one!)
2. Am I enjoying music? (I enjoy nothing when depressed.)
3. Do I love my dogs? (When I'm depressed, my beloved dogs—yes, black ones—are a source of irritation.)

It works for me, and I'm a great believer in doing what feels right. I do take antidepressants, and feel no shame about this whatsoever. I am very slowly trying to reduce the dose, but I know that they have helped me enormously.

When I went into hospital, there was a sign in the foyer saying, 'You Are A Miracle', which at the time I thought was new-age crap. But recently my therapist said to me, 'I was telling my group at the hospital about you today'. I looked at her blankly.

She went on, '. . . about how a year ago you wanted to die, and how now you're happier than you've ever been'. I was amazed to be used as an example of hope to other people who were in despair. It meant so much to me that she said that, and that she told me about it, and to realise that I *am* a miracle.

On medication, the anxiety that had gnawed at my stomach for so long began to disappear. I enjoyed long nights of uninterrupted sleep and, like the blue sky peeping from behind a cloud, a new outlook began to emerge. I do not want to lie to you about the medical 'white dog' however, for it has not been an

entirely clear vista. There have been side-effects and medication changes have been far from pleasant. I am always a little
more tired than the average dog owner, a little hungrier, a
little less sexy. However, for the most part, I can assert that on
the right medication I enjoy uninterrupted walks in the park,
whilst the black dog stays at home in his kennel.

I knew there was no shame in seeing an orthopaedic surgeon if
I had broken my leg; I knew it made sense for my wife to consult
a gynaecologist when birth complications threatened; but to
see a psychiatrist was . . . well, somehow it was demeaning. The
old adage had got through to me: you'd have to mad to see a
psychiatrist!

Whatever the reason, I was ashamed, embarrassed, at least
very reluctant to see a psychiatrist, even when my doctor
suggested that such a move might counter my burgeoning
depression. I thought that to admit to having some sort of
mental illness was to commit professional suicide. I am not sure
how I would have coped with that challenge, but Fate took
a hand.

One of the parents at the school where I worked was a
psychiatrist and one evening he popped his head into my office
to ask me how I was. The answer I gave was guarded, but
somehow he knew that I needed help—and in his own gentle
way led me to realise it.

Funnily enough, making the decision to speak with a
psychiatrist was a very important life lesson in itself—and his
support over the coming years was indispensable. It helped me
to see that a psychiatric illness was not the end of the world as I

knew it. More importantly, it helped me to reach out to others who were also suffering.

My ability to cope and live with depression changed for the better with a simple act of kindness from the mother of an old school friend. She had a son with a long history of mental illness and told my wife of a psychiatrist in the city who might be worth a try. I was sceptical as I'd seen a number of psychiatrists in the public system, and the most common denominator amongst them was their reliance on medications in the treatment of depression.

But as soon as I met him, I knew I liked him and was comfortable talking to him about anything. He seemed genuinely interested in my health and was the first doctor to say he thought he could help me and, more importantly, that I could help myself.

He began by admitting me into hospital to safely wean me off the sedatives I had become addicted to. Soon I was thinking a little more clearly. I was kept on a fairly high dose of antidepressants and remain on them to this day. I take them just like a diabetic takes his insulin. My new shrink then arranged weekly consultations and together we spoke about depression, its causes, why all kinds of people have it, and things I could do to cope and live with it. He gave me tips on being more positive and told me that *I could* rather than *I couldn't*. I had read a few self-help books and thought them to be a lot of crap, but this power of positive thinking he encouraged seems to be helping.

Bob and I have always enjoyed a good argument. When I first went to see him ten years ago, I plopped myself into his chair, short-circuited my mental history and begged for a bottle of sedatives to sleep me across to New Zealand for a holiday.

Bob had other ideas. No drugs. He ran 'Fear of Flying' classes. He suggested I might actually like to stay awake for the flight like everyone else—read a magazine, eat a meal, look out the window . . . Was he mad?

Five years later, when I was no longer coping with even the small things in life, I was back in the chair. This time I begged for a drug-free solution, perhaps a mantra I could repeat that would give me some kind of courage for this shocking new phase. Bob had other ideas. Medication was the chosen way to correct a chemical imbalance.

'You're depressed,' said Bob.

'I'm not,' I said.

Bob is shifting in his seat. He takes a bite of his sandwich and chews in thought. Behind him are his famous purple manila folders containing the laughter and tears of a truckload of loyal patients. Bob has so many patients that he double-books himself every fifteen minutes.

'Tell me what's happening.'

I take a deep breath and the relief of revealing the sad me reduces me to jelly. Through the tears I tell him I really am a very happy person. Great family. Great love. Great job. It's just that I have lost control. I can no longer function as a 'normal' person. I want to stay in bed and hide. I can no longer speak on the phone, order sliced ham at the deli or walk along the shiny floor of the shopping centre without fear consuming me. This hot, whirring, choking fear that makes me want to rip off my shirt and run and run to nowhere in particular. That is the hideous thing about the black dog. He always catches up.

Life is now one long panic which makes life one long depression and no-one can live like that. Bob scribbles a prescription for low-level antidepressants and pushes it towards me.

'Come back and see me in two weeks,' he says.

'Can we make it one?' I say.

I have always loathed the idea of taking tablets on a regular basis. At first I grimaced when I swallowed those bitter pills. Was I that bad? Over time, when I saw they took the edge off the horrors, I came to look on them as friends or, at the very least, foot soldiers in the fight.

One great help has been acceptance. Fear of fear seems absurd when there are graver, more tangible things in the world to be worried about. In the past, the idea that I was going mad, that my secret darkness would be revealed, that I would end up in a 'loony bin' strapped to electric pulses, was irresistible. I confided my dread of flipping out in front of friends. 'So what?' said Bob. 'Even if you did, what would it matter?'

Yes, what *would* it matter?

Now I have my mantra: I am not going mad and the worst always passes. When the dog comes back from the kennels, as I know he always will, I make an effort to look away. I focus on my family and, now my son has started school, his friends and their parents. I volunteer to be class convenor, stagger under the demands of Easter raffles and teachers' birthdays, and thank God I have something valuable to do.

On the nights I cannot sleep, when morbid thoughts sweep around the pillow, I employ my 'lists'. It might be all the capital cities in the world, tennis players currently on the circuit, movie stars in America . . . This may not be yoga, but it is a way of controlling my thoughts, giving me a neutral focus and relaxing. I rarely get beyond fifty—and I always start with Sidney Poitier—before I nod off.

Make it easy on yourself. I try to avoid stressful situations I don't need to be placed in. For example, I will never volunteer to be chairman of a fundraising committee for that would involve public speaking. Even a meeting of four is public speaking. Instead I reward myself with small pleasures: a bubble bath, a lie on the couch at night, a video and an icecream.

There's no reason to talk about the blues with friends. These blues are too big. I am happy to talk about the phobias I am famous for though. I am happy to talk about driving in large circles in order to avoid freeways and bridges. I am happy to talk about the time I taped my presentation for a Spanish tutorial and sat there with the other students taking down my own notes. I am happy to recall the odd 'Xanax moment', ordering a fish dinner on the plane in Frankfurt and waking up to cornflakes in Singapore.

I am happy to try and be happy.

'What's been happening?' asks Bob. He has just returned from Mexico and a series of squat ceramics lines the windowpane.

We talk about art. The trend to abstract work. One of his patients has painted a couple with large Picasso noses that interlock as they kiss upside down. It would look great in the next exhibition. We don't talk about me at all. Bob closes the purple folder in front of him and I realise how soothing the colour is and how Bob is kind of kooky too.

'See you in a month,' he says.

'Can we make it three?' I say.

Day by day my will to live returned. It was like putting bubbles back into flat lemonade. Absolutely nothing else in my life circumstances changed, but on medication I was able to meet the challenges now that the crippling weight of the dog was lifting from my back. In the end, the difference between life and death was so simple. All it took was the smallest sprinkle of a substance to spice up the sluggish intercellular soup stagnating in the synapses of my brain. The surge sparked up a speck of my stricken soul and I not only survived but subsequently went on to shine and am sparkling still.

I am now almost expert at recognising the signs, the first trickle of subterranean waters, which build to accelerating undercurrents. I guess I'm a slow learner, for it wasn't always obvious.

After two years of counselling, and numerous journals filled, the suction of the spiral began to lessen. Well-thumbed self-help books occupied a complete shelf of a bookcase. I had answers. Unpalatable, perhaps, but answers nonetheless.

'You have to realise you'll never be normal,' the psychologist told me during my final session. Normal or not, I was provided with the rudimentary tools for moving on with my life and avoiding prolonged visits to the void.

A visit to my general practitioner offered some hope, but I baulked, immovable on the issue of antidepressants. They were not an option. Having had all control over my situation and circumstances, and most importantly my body, denied me as a child, the adult me would not and could not willingly make that choice, even knowing the depression would continue and most probably regurgitate in the future. I grasped at herbal alternatives: one to encourage substantial sleep, a multivitamin to supplement decreased appetite and an inadequate diet, another to soothe frayed nerves, and yet one more, St John's Wort, for depression. Together, they helped repair the fractured rungs on the ladder out of the void. But it wasn't enough.

Once more, I sought counselling. My first effort was disappointing. Rapport was minimal. The office cancelled the second session, without explanation or apology. I cancelled the fifth, without explanation. I saw little benefit in discussing, interminably, what we might try in future sessions, considering I had serious concerns about surviving this particular ride on the Depression Roller-coaster.

Today, journalling and artwork take precedence over housework during limited time at home, a conscious decision. Herbal remedies sit on the shelf where I will be reminded to take them. Early morning walks, when others, who would force me to adjust the mask, are not yet stirring, get me moving and help ground me in the here and now with gentle action.

458

Often, the most mundane of activities—walking the dog, mowing the lawn—is enough to lift me out of the black hole. However, in the end, I found I could not fight it alone. I had to seek professional help—a psychiatrist and a psychologist too. (You need a good support team to take on such a formidable enemy as depression.) To do this requires a small leap of faith, a throwing away of misconceptions and, most importantly, the loss of a sense of shame. Forget the stigma associated with mental illness. Think of it as an act of courage. A psychologist told me that. 'You are going to a complete stranger and saying, "Please help me",' he said. 'Now that takes guts.'

I picture myself as a clay pot that has been formed with impurities and, when fired, explodes into thousands of pieces. My family and health professionals begin the long and tedious job of trying to put me back together, piece by piece, God love 'em.

After my breakdown and seven and a half long weeks of hospitalisation, thanks to the medical professionals and my partner, there is a new clay pot. It isn't the same as the old one, it's better. By better, I mean that with medication and the deeper understanding I have of depression and its triggers, I am finally experiencing some stability for the first time in my life.

My mother not only saw the glass as half empty; she also saw cracks, smudges and completely the wrong sort of glass.

537

8. Travelling companions
Perspective of family and friends

> Should we get stuck in depression, it is helpful to remember, or have someone point out to us, that it will not last forever.
>
> 583

Depression devastates more lives than that of the individual sufferer. Many of the writers spoke from the perspective of a carer. Depression's fall-out affects parents, partners, children and friends, permeating the lives of all who love and care for a person with a mental illness.

> However dreadful the black dog is for its owner, it's almost as difficult for relatives who live with the owner. If you love someone, you have to learn to get along with their 'pet' as well.
>
> 59

> Living with depression is a journey—not only for the sufferer, but also for the loved ones. There are no words powerful enough to describe this demon. A depressed person can be

very frustrating and uncomfortable to be around . . . You
long for them to be back to normal.

For friends and family, adjusting to the impact of someone
else's depressive episodes is a rocky process. As already highlighted, an individual with a mood disorder can go for years
without their condition being diagnosed, and even then
may refuse to accept that there is a problem. As a result,
family and friends are often exposed to troubling, confusing
and oppressive behaviours, without being aware they are
dealing with a tractable illness. An unfortunate side-effect of
mental illness is behaviour that can be out-of-character and
hurtful. Action taken and words said during the slough of a
depressed mood or in the midst of an exhilarating high often
leave an enduring emotional scar. For this reason, it is important for carers, as much as possible, to separate the illness
from the person they love, and keep perspective on the
mood distortions of the illness.

Depressive illness is inherently isolative and absorbing,
leaving those who care on the periphery, trying to manage
their lives in the void remaining. Many carers write of their
anger, frustration and disappointment in losing the person
they love to the wilderness of depression.

Until you have either suffered from this condition, or
been associated with someone who has, there is really no
way of grasping what it is and everything that goes along
with it. I was one of those non-graspers up until one and
a half years ago. It's as though the person you knew has

disappeared and sometimes it seems like they will never return.

47

It is a complicated and difficult task to be the one destined to help from the sideline. Enormous reserves of strength are needed to support someone who is struggling and in pain, especially knowing that, ultimately, you are unable to provide a fix or cure, or 'magic wand' to make the illness disappear.

> For me, her mother, I would love nothing better than to cast a spell over her and right the imbalance that has caused this debilitating disease. I have, at times, questioned 'Why me?' But it's not about me. It's about understanding and the support that I can give when needed. As much as I would like to change her life, I know she is the only one who can control this disease, with the assistance of medication and therapy. I only hope she will find the ongoing strength and that life will eventually get better. As long as I am here, I will remain her best friend. There is hope, I know there is.

368

The complex 'burden of sympathy' (Karp, 2001) in dealing with someone else's mental health problems is certainly not an easy load to carry. Carers are confronted with their own emotions that can revolve around feelings of grief, guilt, anger, bitterness and sorrow. Crucially, carers must be careful not to lose their identity to the enveloping quicksand of the illness. They must learn to set boundaries to protect their own lives, and sense of themselves, from engulfment.

I am frozen. Stuck somewhere in the middle of selfishness and wanting to help. The worst part: it's always about them—often you feel like a shadow.

420

My heart was torn. I became very lonely, confused and angry, constantly on edge and sad, not knowing how my husband would behave. I lost my identity as I became engrossed in looking after him and shielding my family.

436

Family and friends may feel transported into an alien land, with no road map to show them how to guide their family member or friend to solid ground. Propelled along, care-givers are often forced to cope out of pure necessity. Their own emotional journey often parallels the chaotic moods of the person with depression, and it can take years to learn the most effective strategies to keep from sinking with them.

We were in a tug-of-war—he would struggle to pull me down to join him in the pit, but I knew if he won, we were both lost.

250

While unconditional love and unwavering belief are the ideal, it is vital for carers to recognise that maintaining such a high level of unwavering support is not easy and not always possible. In the face of what can be a recurrent and long-term illness, parameters of obligations and commit-ment need to be negotiated. In fact, one of the challenges that carers face is to accept that their family member or friend's depression is not their battle to fight and that there is only so much they can do to help.

> We realise that we, like so many people, had no under-standing of the depths of despair and absolute suffering. In our muddled way we were coping, hanging on. We grieved for the loss of our dreams for this intelligent, beautiful daughter. We replaced our dreams with unconditional love . . . It's a slow and painful experience to work through, but we are richer for it. We have learnt that it is her illness, not ours, and she must be trusted to deal with it herself. 566

The following narratives highlight how depression affects different relationships in different ways. For children with a parent with a mental illness, the consequences can impact on developing healthy bonds and trust. For partners, it can cause great strain. For parents, it can be a heartbreaking burden of pain and guilt.

Yet the most important message in this chapter is how precious this support is in the fight against depression. When people lose their way and can no longer trust their own thoughts or perceptions, family and friends can be the mirror to remind them of who they once were. Love, constant remind-ers of the individual's significance and assurances that 'it will pass' can help pilot the way through depression's wasteland.

> People who suffer with the sufferer often have clarity of mind that helps enable the loved one to replace the curved

and distorted mirror with one that provides a more accurate reflection. We shouldn't walk away from this type of cancer of the mind.

556

As children growing up, we enjoyed watching cowboy movies. I don't know why but we always expected at least one scene where someone got caught in quicksand. It made simple sense if it was one of the Baddies who died this way. It added drama if a Goodie fell in and was saved. Lying on the lounge-room floor, clutching for the rope thrown from an armchair, we would act out these scenes dozens of times, pretending we were being sucked into the quicksand. We thought only momentarily about how it would feel being consumed by this silent blackness.

These cowboy movies of the 1960s seem so long ago (I am showing my age) but the image of the quicksand victim returned to me in recent years as I watched my son suffer with depression.

Like the pool of quicksand, it is hard for me to say with precision when Jack's depression started. It is not like breaking an arm or a leg. I can't point to a day or a month or a year when he became depressed. Somewhere along the way it took hold of him. It was somewhere after the magic moment of his birth. It was somewhere after the days when he was a baby and people in the street would stop and comment on his winning smile. And it was somewhere before his late teens when he consulted our general practitioner and was prescribed antidepressants.

He was, and is, a child with a variety of interests. He enjoys academic pursuits. He enjoys physical pursuits. He enjoys artistic pursuits. He has performed well in all three. He is physically healthy, and at the age of twenty-three he still has his winning smile. My friends often comment on his good looks. They say he has sexy eyes. I don't paint this picture to boast about him, but more to set the background against which he struggled with his depression and I struggled to understand it and how to cope with it.

I used to look at him and wonder how a child with so much talent and so much opportunity could fail to find contentment. But depression, like quicksand, is not selective with its victims. It wraps its dark and smothering cloak around people regardless of their intelligence, beauty, talents, social standing, physical prowess or financial position.

During his last two to three years at school, Jack seemed isolated from his peers. Did they see this? I don't know. He went through the motions of school sporting activities and the like, but drew little companionship from this. He spent hours reading. He devoured the writings of James Joyce, Truman Capote, Scott Fitzgerald and Joseph Conrad, and then read whatever he could lay his hands on about the authors. Why was he drawn to the works of troubled artists with their bleak messages? As a mother, I admired his inquiring mind but, also as a mother, I wanted him to enjoy the simplicity and freedom of childhood. I wonder now if I was too quick to praise the intellectual rather than seeing that he used it as a shield.

Jack and I talked about his unhappiness. We did not refer to it as depression. Yes, he was depressed but I thought it was transitory. I thought that, in the main, it was because he was a child who found school limiting and socialising with his age group difficult. I gave it other labels. I desperately wanted him to be happier. I know it is a motherhood statement, but I lived his pain with him. It hurt to hear him sobbing in his bedroom. I would try to comfort him. Talk him through his lowest moments. Rationalise. Give advice. Stroke his forehead. Whilst the quicksand pulled him in a downward spiral, I tried to throw him the rope from the armchair.

Then, and now, I ask: am I somehow responsible for his suffering? Is it something I did or didn't do? Why has this happened to him? I can read about depression and family histories and genetic links. I can intellectualise about causation, but, as his mother, could I have made a difference?

Rather than Jack being able to chase it away, the black dog moved in and dominated his life after he left school. The debilitating periods became more frequent and intense. They would drain away his energy. He talked of giving up. He could not see that his future would ever be any different. He had been a prisoner held in the quicksand of depression for as long as he could remember and he was tired. He craved just one day when he could switch off the tormenting tape in his head. I felt powerless and at times fatigued by his suffering.

Jack's first hospitalisation for depression came nine months after leaving school. He was overseas. Sadly the black dog is an international traveller. We had been in regular contact, but still his desperate call came from out of the blue. 'Mum, I need help.' I won't forget the pleading in his voice nor the fear I felt. He was in the quicksand and I was not there to throw the rope to him. I was frightened that I would lose him.

His second and third hospitalisations came a year later when he was back in Sydney.

No matter how broadminded you think you are, it is confronting to have your child admitted to a psychiatric hospital. I have a public and a private life. I am the product of an upbringing where you did not wear your heart on your sleeve. I was taught that, in adversity, stoicism is a virtue. So despite my training as a social worker and a lawyer, despite my baby boomer upbringing, despite my love of my family and my absolute love of my struggling son, I was only able to tell two friends about Jack's admission to hospital. My family and work colleagues did not know.

Why was it a secret? Early on, Jack had asked me not to tell people about his constant struggle. He did not want to be the topic of conversation because of it. He feared he would be diminished in other people's eyes, even in the family. To be honest, I was comfortable with this request. I found it so hard to talk about it to others anyway. Partly because I wondered what their reaction would be. Partly because I am my mother's daughter and we hide our pain. And partly because I saw it as Jack's privacy about which only he could make decisions. I rationalised our secrecy.

In retrospect, I was wrong to do this. Secrecy about depression simply fuels the fire of despair for everyone involved. Pretending everything is all right closes the door on support, whereas disclosure has healing qualities and spreads a safety net beneath the sufferer. But it is easier to know these truths than to act on them. I am learning to act.

It was fortunate that through his dark haze, Jack was always able to ask for help. Even today, as I write, a friend of mine five hundred kilometres away is burying her son; a wonderful and much-loved young man who took his own life. At times, when Jack was at his lowest, I worried that he might do the same. If he was late home or late up, my mind would be tormented by such thoughts, relieved only by the sound of him closing the front door or opening his bedroom door. Help and death can be seconds apart.

What an all-powerful thing is this depression that it can torture a person so much that the human instinct for self-preservation is overridden. The taunt by some to 'pull up your socks' fails to appreciate the enormity of the blackness, the despair and the exhaustion that engulfs the sufferer. Everyday tasks can be too hard. It took me time to understand. It took me time to see that Jack's hours of sleeping or video watching were respite for him from the struggle of each day. It looks mindless to the outsider but it is restorative in a sense. If you stay still in the quicksand, you might not sink so fast.

Through years of psychiatric treatment, anger, fear, resolution, impatience, self-doubt, tears, humour, strength, openness, willpower, courage, understanding and gradual acceptance, Jack has chased his black dog towards its kennel. But it is still there in the backyard. The dark periods have become far less frequent and far less intense. Will he ever be totally free of it? I do not know. Will the dark days return? I do not know. What is important is that he knows his life is now different. He knows he can be free of the torment.

For the moment, most of his body is out of the quicksand. Whilst I will always be there to stand on the chair and throw him the rope, for now I can put it away.

324

Depression doesn't run in my family; it crawls on all fours from the bedroom to the bathroom at 4 a.m.

525

I have known him for fifty years, yet I hardly know him at all. Periodically he becomes a stranger. I call this intruder the 'Fire Breathing, Soul Destroying Dragon', who roars in and changes our lives and the lives of friends and family. The Dragon breathes its fiery breath, devouring all serenity.

All he wants to do is escape. No hugs or reassurance on my part can help. I have to be careful not to make the situation worse by saying the wrong thing. The angry rejection breaks my heart and I realise it's happening all over again for the 500th time. How I hate this angry, violent Dragon.

I refrain from disturbing him. I have learnt over the years that this is the best thing to do, as he needs to be alone. I just get on with what I have to do now and wait. Wait for the Dragon to be gone and for us to be happy again. Gradually our lives get back on an even keel, but each time it happens I find it hard to forget.

Life goes on. Love holds us together. Sometimes I wonder if we will continue to cope as we both grow older. I know I am less tolerant as I have heard the same excuses and insults directed at me for far too long.

204

The bottomless depth of suffering I encountered in those green eyes wrenched at my heart. Had I missed all the signs? Guilt and frustration chased each other through my subconscious. My fault! I should have been more vigilant, more aware of his slide toward the dark side, his inability to fight the call of the blackness once again.

We need help. It's happened again. Help this precious man, this husband, this dad, this granddad, this son, this special person loved by so many.

Gradually, slowly emerging from the fog, he comes back to us. Little by little we see snippets of the whole him. He will be fine.

I live with five men. There's 'Mr Under-Control', 'Mr On-the-Edge', 'Mr Out-of-Control', 'Mr High-as-a-Kite' and 'Mr Depths-of-Despair'.

Fortunately, Mr Under-Control is the main guy around our house, but the others, who are only temporary residents/intruders, still make themselves at home from time to time.

I have lived with this assortment of the one man (my beautiful husband) for almost six years. He is bipolar.

Thanks to one of these intruders, Mr Depths-of-Despair, I often have to watch my competent, witty and vibrant friend experience a metamorphic event and become a crumbling, under-confident, desperate mess in a very short space of time. I am witness to the 'dog' moving into his soul. It invades his whole being. His eyes go distant and become very, very sad and his posture slumps. Withdrawing from us all, he does not want to talk or be talked to. In these times, no amount of reasoning or hugging will help.

Three Christmases ago, when I was heavily pregnant with our second child, his black dog turned up. For two days leading up to Christmas Day, apart from trips to the toilet, he was unable to leave the refuge of one of the rooms in our house. He wanted it darkened and he wrapped himself in blankets saying he was cold even though it was thirty degrees outside. When he did emerge, he was almost uncontactable he was so low.

My coping strategy at that time was to carry on as normal. I made a nice Christmas dinner for the three of us and hoped that it would entice him out of wherever he had gone.

Of course this did nothing. The chemical in his head that drags him to this dreadful place is a stubborn beast and always makes sure he does his time.

In our early days, when I first began encountering this 'other guy', I used to find myself being pulled along and, to a certain degree, falling too. It seemed so reasonable to be depressed. We were poor, owned nothing and seemed always to be struggling through life. However, I have learned since that 'reasonable' is not a word to associate with bipolar.

The depressions I have witnessed are like a cloud of doom. His mood is stuck as if thick glue has been poured into his head. A glue that will, however, in time, weaken and dissipate.

Through experience, and by sometimes doing the wrong thing, I have come to find my key coping tool: patience. Over time these periods will and do pass. I know when I see and feel them coming that there will be a hard few days ahead, but they will end and the man I recognise will return. And he will feel possibly embarrassed, usually exhausted and always truly sorry that he has put his family through such a painful experience.

Two other incredibly important coping tools are our beautiful children. Initially, my husband protested about having children. He believed that with his condition he would make a terrible father. Of course, the opposite is the case. They adore him and he them. Nothing can bring the shine back to an otherwise shitty day like the sound of them calling him 'Daddy'.

And together I believe we bring him more than that. By standing by him and accepting him as he is, we give him a gift that I believe all those who suffer from mental illness require: a true sense of self-worth.

The illness is only part of the man I have chosen as my life partner, but it is not something that I abhor or dread. Instead I consider myself lucky. We have a wonderfully close relationship and a very productive life. To me, he is not only an amazingly strong human being for surviving the turmoils and chaos his condition has created, but also for becoming the caring, giving and unique soul that I love.

Together we have learnt, and are learning, that even with Mr Depths-of-Despair and all the others in our life, we can survive anything life throws at us.

567

Managing and living with depression demands more than one person taking the leash. For a number of years I watched the black dog lead my wife around, not really understanding WHAT was dragging her into deep sadness, sitting on her chest, immobolising her.

Carrying the depression has strained our relationship to breaking point. I admired, respected and loved this woman but I didn't like what depression did to her.

556

When Pa goes off into the garden, pulls some weeds, and has a beer on his own under the frangipani tree, I don't begrudge him running away. Every other day he slices banana for Nan's cereal. Threads her earrings through her earlobes. Washes her hair over the sink. Guides her through her own famous lemon cheesecake recipe.

He loves her with all of his heart—has done for nearly fifty years—but it can't be easy on him. He's had to watch the flame-haired young woman he fell in love with, as they danced the jitterbug on the Palais Royale dance floor, slip away. Had to stand useless, despite working himself to tears trying to help, as the black dog nipped at his wife's heels.

205

Over the years we've learnt to live with the depression. It's not easy at times. Sometimes we say things and wish we'd engaged our brain first. We are only human and do not have an instruction manual. So strap on the guilt backpack—in the middle of carrying the weight comes your own life to live. I do wish I didn't have to cope with it. But, if it's bad for me, I cannot even begin to imagine her turmoil.

87

He needs to know we love and support him. We must not blame him. We will search until we find help . . . What it took from him, he has more than reclaimed. Where the suffering of a child is involved, I can't say 'it's worth it', but I don't want to change the outstanding person he has become.

511

Sometimes it's still not easy talking about my father. It's not because I'm ashamed or embarrassed about his battles with depression, but because this affliction has the awful power to corrode my memories, like a small black termite gnawing away at those recollections I adore. Those recollections that define where I came from, who I am, the values I believe in.

It threatened to overtake parts of me, my memories and happiness—I unreasonably blamed him and not his condition. I've realised that's one of the curses of this illness—that it has an insidious power to affect not only the present, but to cloud happiness of the past.

It has taken Dad's illness to make me see and understand these incredible traits in my family, some of the most admirable we all possess: resilience, perseverance, dedication, understanding. They are the things that had lain dormant within me, cajoled and teased out by the need to support. In a strange way, Dad's depression disguised an underlying gift—the opportunity to rally round and understand each other.

Even though it may have taken the affliction of depression to make me fully understand the power of love and family, it is—reluctantly, resentfully, begrudgingly—something I may have to eventually thank depression for.

335

Her smiles were my sunrises. But the bad moods always returned. I spent years navigating my way through the unpredictable turbulence of our life, riding the highs and somehow surviving the lows. At school I did my best to fit in. I remember longing for the kind of lunches packed by the cake-baking mothers of all the other kids . . . There are a number of people who sheltered me from the storm at the centre of my life— they are the spiritual buoys that saved me from drowning in those seas.

What I have learnt is that, for me, there is no cure, but there is an opportunity to know myself better.

115

I am grieving for the loss of my mother. I am a little boy held in my mother's arms inside a man's body who is not quite sure who this doped psychotic woman is.

One minute he was my hero and someone who I wanted to embrace, the next he was someone terrifying who I wanted to hide from and avoid altogether. I remember being confused by his symptoms. I realised that unmanaged depression has a devastating impact on people's lives. Without treatment, it destroys friendships, turns marriages upside-down, tears families apart.

There is hope. Beating the illness takes time and is often a process of four steps forward and two back. Support is crucial. We all need help, someone to believe in us. It's important that we stand united and help deal with life's adversity.

This was my family seventeen years ago: my wife and the three delightful seedlings we had grown from the germ of our love and passion. They were happy—they were all happy—and trust was written on their faces in the big, bold, beautiful text of laughing eyes and smiles that knew no shame or dark secrets. Like most dads whose happy infants had been traded for young adults, the longing to go back was palpable: cravings made far worse by understanding the effect my mental illness had on our three collections of trust and love.

I have bipolar disorder. It had mostly shown itself through the manic or 'up' phases of the illness. Here, on the sometimes flickering tape, is my rapid-fire wit and the ability to do and think many things at once. At the time, my capacity to devote long hours to a variety of projects was legendary. I thought fast, talked fast. Creativity and giftedness sat comfortably beside ambition and the belief that my destiny was greatness.

But I let the manic drive for excellence pervade every part of my life. In doing so, I crushed those around me, trading on all the love deposits I had earlier put in their emotional bank. As the balances went into overdraft, the mania came less often and I lived in a black well of depression with 'the voices' as my constant companions. Five auditory hallucinations that plotted my demise, encouraged my insanity and even urged me to kill my wife. They were a sure sign of my times.

My wife's gift was the courageous way she shielded our children for so long from the strange things Daddy was now doing. Long hours of disassociation, where my outward responses were a blank stare and a motionless body. Fits of unrestrained white-heat anger whose physical manifestations destroyed inanimate objects. The same anger, when fed through a razor-sharp tongue, caused damage to my wife that was even greater. In time, even she could not prevent exposure to my bipolar radiation and for a few years they lived in a state of constant retreat to the fall-out shelter she provided at the first sign of Armageddon.

I became delusional and angry. Those now-older faces of my children cried for what they had lost and, appropriately, for what they missed. My wife, always my strongest supporter, cried in confusion and in her own anger at being placed in that impossible gulf between her great loves: her husband and her children.

As the millennium turned, I was gone to a world of psychosis and black mania: three suicide attempts, a wrong diagnosis and therefore wrong medication, and a world too confusing and far too painful to live in. It was the last of those love and trust deposits—those my wife held—which saw me through.

In literally my last stroke on the surface before releasing myself to the welcoming, numbing blackness below, I found an answer.

Using the internet—mostly American sites back then—I discovered that I had something known: bipolar disorder. In that moment of realisation that I wasn't alone, that others felt and suffered as I did and that someone knew what to do about it—in that moment I found hope.

As a person who loves a chat, it would be convincing to say therapy came easy for me. It didn't! Pride, intellect and stubbornness were negative influences, but again I was lucky. My therapist was patient, professional and well-versed in my problem. He claimed I was fascinating! It took fourteen months of weekly sessions and a few follow-up adjustments but it worked.

I am compliant with medication—not something bipolars find easy—but I have good reasons. First, it puts me on a level playing field. It's not a cure—there is none—but it provides me with a chance to use management techniques like cognitive behavioural therapy that give me a fighting chance at life. Second, my medication is adjusted so I still cycle but not to the dangerous extremities at the very edges of sanity. This means benefits like creativity—for me, writing—are still accessible and although the thinking takes a little more work, it provides me with more reflection time. I still suffer the depressive parts of the cycle but my wife and I have worked out a system called 'rescue your day'. On bad days, the aim is to get out of bed and complete one task that takes you out of the house and then celebrate it. Sometimes it's as small as bringing the bills in from the letterbox but on a bad day, that's a hell of an achievement. The third reason for compliance is survival. I don't want to go back where I was. I have too many great things ahead of me.

Rebuilding those emotional bank accounts in the past four years has been more difficult than you could imagine. You don't just announce one day that you are well and everyone jumps aboard the love-and-mung-bean train to happiness, flowers festooning their hair. My loved ones have been damaged. The stresses and strains of watching and living with a mentally ill father are greatest on those least equipped to cope. Even though your children never sacrifice love as they learn to survive, trust is lost. Gradually it will return. But as they were patient, so I will have to be. When your dad would rather kill himself than stay with you, trust is scattered like seeds in a strong wind.

My wife and I are rediscovering our relationship but there isn't enough fat in it to take anything for granted. She has suffered and although she knows my illness was the culprit, it looked and sounded like me at the time. She had to become strong and independent and it's taking time, effort and understanding for us to safely merge back to the unified body of the 'one' made from two.

We have to remember the fun and love and trust we once had—justification enough for creating that singular entity again.

143

To be the child of a depressed parent is difficult—as a child I was furious at her behaviour (withdrawal). Where does that anger go?

Watching a person unravel is another painful lesson. I took every opportunity to be with positive people outside the house.

For years I was angry at my sister, and perhaps a part of me will always be, for how she disrupted my life. I could go on and recall the countless times she brought me to tears and the countless times my family would be in feud. The countless occurrences that even now make me cautious to believe or trust in others. It's still a constant struggle, forgetting the past and moving forward. As a child I could not read beyond her actions and see the sadness. I now realise she has an illness.

It is true that bipolar disorder affects the entire family, not just the sufferer. But what I have learnt through growing up was that it was 100 per cent more difficult for my sister. I am proud of her now that she has realised she cannot do it alone and is seeking help.

While it was my husband's shoulder on which the black dog was perched, it often raised its ugly head and growled at me. While obviously the person suffering is going through their own hell, their partners and family suffer as well, and fight their own battles with the invisible dog. While I was not the ill one, the black dog was most certainly breathing heavily over me too.

I found that while he was working his way through the process with wonderful assistance from health professionals, I was suddenly expected to snap my fingers and forgive and forget and pretend I had not been through a difficult period. I felt, as a partner, I was not getting the support from the health profession that I too needed. This was the most difficult part of dealing with his depression—there was no closure on this dark period for me.

It helped to have contact with other people who understood. When I couldn't sleep, I found that chat rooms on the Web and bulletin boards for those with mood disorders were really helpful. A family friend with bipolar disorder was a wonderful source of ideas in 'being nice to yourself' and being patient with the healing process.

My family were useless at first—so hard to talk to about it. 'You're not depressed, you're just a bit down! You're just not a depressed kind of person—you've always been so positive. You'll be right!' However, they learnt and eventually became a wonderful source of support. They continued reaching out to me, creating opportunities for me to get out and interact, and kept on reaching out even when I was quick to anger or clearly not enjoying myself. Often, Depressed Me was being a complete bitch, but Real Me was in there somewhere, slowly waking up. My family learnt to ignore the personality changes, the anger and the restlessness. They were very patient, cooked meals and helped maintain a routine.

My mother suffers from bipolar depression. She changes in front of me at times, jumping seemingly out of nowhere into a miserable state. She may feel upset thinking the world is out to get her, or she might feel frustrated and angry with the pressures of life.

When she is in this state, it is impossible to change her mood or her opinion, so I don't try to. Instead I try to encourage the good things that are happening, trying to spot the silver lining in the cloud.

I tell her that no matter what anyone else thinks, I will always love her and that she will always have me to confide in. At the time it may not mean much because she is suffering from her illness. But I know that later, when she is feeling better, she can look back at what I said and appreciate it.

Naturally I worry sometimes, when she may be crying or yelling. This is because it scares me to see my mum like that. I am only fourteen and so I don't really understand much of what is going on. It confuses me that someone who is my greatest role model can just break down sometimes. But I know that if I get depressed, it will only make things worse for her.

So I try to act calm. I ignore Mum when she yells at me or when she starts putting herself down. I can't let those things affect me, it's the one thing I do remember from the brochures and articles she has given to me. I know that all I have to do is support her through the bad times and try not to take it out on myself.

Sometimes Mum's bipolar becomes so bad she has to go to hospital. I feel she is safe there because there are doctors who can help her better than I possibly can. The only time when this has been a concern to me was when some doctors actually came to my house to see how Mum was going. I felt something serious must have been going on for them to come into our house.

Mum sometimes tells me that I shouldn't have to carry the burden of her depression. Sometimes she will get confused and tell me that I shouldn't have to deal with it and that I am better off living with another family member. To me, she is not a burden, she is my mum and I love her even when she is bipolar. I know that sometimes I have to make decisions for us. I do the best thing for her. And I know that living with her is the best thing.

She always tells me that her kids are her life. So what would happen if I were to live with someone else? I know it would only make her depression worse and I know that it would probably ruin my life at the same time.

As long as I am the best son I can be and help Mum through her sickness, I know that I will not break into depression and I can make my mum feel proud of me.

318

You think you have the black dog under control. Sure, as long as you live under the same roof, you know that the black dog will always be with her, will always be skulking in the shadows somewhere. But you have it house-trained. You are firm. You keep your own heart tight on a leash.

It's all about rules, all about routine.

Firstly, exercise. It is crucial to keep her moving, all the time. The black dog likes nothing better than to slouch, it curls into grooves on the couch, indents on the bed. And once she nuzzles in beside it, it flips over, presses down on top of her until her legs are heavy forgotten things and there is not enough energy to turn herself over, let alone leave the house. Until the only things moving are things behind her eyes, worries and memories whirr and churn inside, hopes helter-skelter down her oesophagus, fears thud on her aorta.

Once the black dog is sprawled on top of her, it can be difficult to remove. So you must keep her moving all the time. Brisk walks, morning swims, aerobics in front of daytime TV. Buy a treadmill if you can.

Talking is also important. Fill the silences. It doesn't matter what comes out, whether it's how your football team is going to clean up on Saturday or who set fire to who at school. The words aren't important. It's the making of sound waves that matters.

Because the black dog loves silence. You can come home into an empty room, a room in which pins would line up to drop, and you can hear it whispering to her. Filling up the silence with 'if only', 'why' and 'why can't you be'. And sometimes it speaks in her voice and sometimes it doesn't, but always the words sound like razors. And you try to make your voice as soft as it can go, try rubbing her back and saying nice things, but even if the room is quiet you know she can't hear you.

Once the black dog starts barking, it is difficult to muzzle. But if you keep talking she will never hear it. Beware, you may wear your larynx out: it is advisable to keep a supply of soothing lozenges at hand.

Thirdly, avoid mess. Try and keep on top of household cleaning. The black dog is particularly untidy. The mess it leaves is loud and ugly—the stacked dishes and mouldy veggies silently judge and condemn her. And once she feels ashamed by them, she cannot move and you are stuck in trap one: lethargy.

Scour and scrub every surface regularly. Replace germs with flowers and smiley faces, especially in the colour yellow. Radiate happy thoughts. Say 'I love you' and mean it: this is like 'Fee Fi Fo Fum' to the black dog.

Keep her dressed at all times. The black dog is especially fond of her dressing gown; it longs to see the neighbours call by at 4 p.m. and find her picking cornflakes out of her nightie. Set up an emergency make-up kit at the front door, so that when she leaves the house you can touch up the folds under her eyes, you can gloss over any sags and stretches.

Lastly, alcohol. This is obvious. Keep the black dog away from all kinds of alcohol, even if it starts with just a splash of wine. You know what alcohol does to her. It isn't nice.

You do all these things. These are your rules, your routine. You keep your eye on the black dog, the reluctant lodger and loafer in your house. You think you have it under control.

Except there are some times when the rules have exceptions, when 'i' follows 'e', when the straight line is not the fastest way. Sometimes you keep her moving, keep her busy like a spinning top. She looks great. There are no stacked dishes or strewn clothes, she is wearing make-up and not the dressing gown, her smile stretches like the sun. And still the black dog whooshes in and whumps her under anyway. And sometimes you can be talking all the time, lots of funny stories and interesting gossip, 'I love you' and 'You're great' sprinkled in like M&M's. But you can see that it's just noise to her, you can hear her shut the doors in her ears.

And sometimes you can fill the room with daffodils dancing with daffodils, with candy canes and choirs of happy babies laughing, and it only makes her sadder.

You can feel so helpless, like you are watching the black dog grow. Until there is nothing in the house but the black dog—it is a large, inflatable monster filling every good space and nice word and safe corner. You want to puncture it, punch it, kick it, strangle it. You want to kill it for good. You want to shake her, slap her, scream at her that you want your mother back, to pull herself together, to move on. You cannot believe she lets it win like this.

Because there are so many great dogs inside her—fierce strong Alsatians that would defend you till the death, stupid lovely labradors that tell you bedtime stories, primping poodles, little terriers that have a joke for every occasion, beautiful Dalmatians that don't have to say anything when you're sad—all of these are inside her, all of these live here sometimes but now she is only listening to that manky, dirty thing.

It would be easier if there was a rule book. If there was a tablet that could make the black dog disappear all the time, a word that could abracadabra it away. If time were a medicine that came with a money-back guarantee.

But, of course, I don't have any magic solutions. Sometimes the practical things help, sometimes listening does, sometimes neither works. I can't claim to really know what it feels like to have a black dog pressing down on you, I can only try to understand. And perhaps this is where we come to some sort of reconciliation.

Maybe this means not giving it biscuits and throwing sticks with it, but not kicking over the bowl either. Sometimes just acknowledging it helps. Writing it down, talking about it without shame, at a regular volume, with family, doctors, other people. Realising that sometimes when you try to help, you are being patronising; that sometimes when somebody needs you, you are oblivious. Realising that sometimes people need to go through darkness, need to stop moving to know what's important.

Realising that the black dog might always be here, might always be beside her, might always be one of the barks in the cacophony, but that it won't always be the loudest, and that if you don't answer it back, it will never stop.

Living with depression is looking to the future and seeing only a void. Worrying that one day I simply will not have the energy to fight on for even one more moment. Many times I have been swamped with the overwhelming fact that I have to battle this blackness for the rest of my life.

It's on days like this that my coping mechanism saves my life, my support network switches into gear: a friend who also suffers, to tell me she knows just how I feel; a life partner to tell me that everything will be fine and that he will always be here for me; and parents who understand what I am going through and step in to pick up my slack—all of this without judgement.

Depression is an extremely lonely disease; the nature of the beast is that as sufferers, we tend to withdraw into ourselves and away from those that we love. It is so very easy to let our lives close in around us, and make no effort to carry on with normality. The problem with this is that it is so very hard to swim back to the top of that very deep hole. I think that without a strong support network, the struggle to get out of the hole would be virtually impossible.

I have a dear friend who, unfortunately, also suffers from this insidious disease, and often when I have struggled to stem the tide of an oncoming bout of depression, it is she who I call first. Probably because I know that it's OK to tell her that I failed and that it's back. She will never ask, 'What can you possibly have to be sad about?', because she knows that I don't need a reason to be sad, I just am. She understands when I need to cry, or when the drugs make even a basic conversation almost impossible, so she will do the talking for me. She is someone who, during better times, I can talk to about this disease and I know without doubt that she really understands. Talking to her eases my mind a little: she is the only person who can allay some of the guilt that comes with every battle. I can only hope that I am as important to her as a support as she is to me.

I have a partner, who has lived through almost as much hell as I have, except he lives on the outside looking in. He is my strength during the worst of times, he holds me up, he makes my excuses, he looks after our children, and he carries on with all of our lives when I cannot possibly take another step. All of this, he does with conviction and without bitterness, judgement or anger. In my darkest moments, he tells me he will always love me no matter what and that I must carry on because he will not be without me under any circumstances. I thank God every day for bringing this man into my life and I cannot imagine how I ever would have survived without him.

I have parents with whom my family lives, in an extended family. Having a daughter who is a lifelong sufferer of depression, my parents have come to recognise the symptoms and signals, sometimes well before I realise myself. They will relieve me of as much everyday burden and pressure as they can, to try and make my life easier. They provide my children with unconditional love, when I am simply not capable. They help my husband with the things at hand as much as they can, and most of all they make many allowances for my behaviour during my struggles and never have they questioned me. They simply smile and welcome me back when I am ready to climb out of the hole.

I cannot begin to imagine how I would fare with this disease without my support network. I have countless things to thank them for, but the most important thing is that they do all this without anger or bitterness. They know that I do not choose this for my life and they accept that there is little I can do to control it. Regardless of how hard it has been, or may be in the future, I know that I can count on these people to be there when I really need them. They have saved my life in the past and undoubtedly will do so again. They are so very important, I could not live without them. **276**

My father: I am told that I get my depression from him. I don't know if this is true but I do know that he was a seriously melancholy fellow, but was always 'too smart' to seek help from anyone else. He did not survive and his short life ended badly. I can't say that I treated him very well when I was growing up. He seemed to recognise in me a kindred spirit, but I had no desire to look into his mirror and avoided him as much as I could. I wanted my dad to be a jokester, a larrikin, a good-time guy. What he was frightened and threatened me. Looking back, though, I can admit that he actually helped me by showing an example I was afraid to follow. **171**

Living with depression is a journey—not only for the sufferer but also for the loved ones. There are no words powerful enough to describe this demon. Its tentacles reach out, it takes the backbone from the strong. It comes knocking on the door via grief, torment, past wrongs, memories, illnesses, circumstances, hurts and harms; and in our weaknesses, when it knocks, it is welcome. Beware its fierce grip!

When Mum was first diagnosed with depression, it is probably true that Dad and I were relieved. At last we knew what was wrong with her. Little did we know the battle that lay ahead. Looking back, we have all come a long way. Sure, Mum was diagnosed, but what next? No-one sat Dad and me down and explained what depression was. We were ignorant, we knew nothing—just like most of the population. Mistakenly, we thought that the 'happy pills' were going to be the wonder drug, the answer to Mum's problems. It (the recovery) couldn't happen fast enough for us. How wrong we were—this was just the beginning. We later learned that whilst medication is important it is just one part of the jigsaw puzzle.

One startling reality was how alone we were—except for a few courageous and compassionate health care practitioners and friends. One of the greatest difficulties in living with the black dog is dealing with the prejudice and lack of understanding. For the sufferers and their carers it seems that there is very little public sympathy. This is despite the fact that depression can be debilitating and it can take years to recover.

The unknown is very frightening. However, we came to realise that the more you know, the less helpless you feel. I recommend to all those living with it to learn all you can about depression, develop positive ways to cope, understand what it does, and be supportive and encouraging. It is important to really try and understand how your loved one has to struggle to get through each day. Try not to be overwhelmed by the illness. Above all, do not judge them. Depression is treatable—there is a light at the end of the tunnel—but recovery takes time.

Disappointingly, even as Mum was discharged from hospital, neither Dad nor I were told what to expect, what we should or shouldn't do, or what to be aware of. Living with the black dog isn't easy. The struggle within every depressed person is agonising. You long for them to be back to normal. You feel inadequacy, sadness, anger, hopelessness and despair. A depressed person can be very frustrating and uncomfortable to be around. They really need love, patience and understanding. It has been said that loving or befriending a depressed person can be a bit like hugging a porcupine. Remind yourself often that your loved one has not chosen to be depressed. Go that extra mile time and time again, although sometimes nothing seems to work! Sometimes they act completely self-absorbed or have no appreciation for anything you do to help.

Be prepared, this illness evokes a lot of guilt. I, too, needed counselling to come to terms with Mum's condition. With reluctance and difficulty, I came to the startling realisation that I am not responsible for the happiness of everyone around me. There was nothing I could do to remove Mum's depression. No-one told me, I found out the hard way, but it is very important for carers who are trying to cope with a loved one with a mental illness to also put up their hand and ask for help. Some months later, I was confiding my anxieties to our GP, who looked across the desk and said to me, 'Your mother will get better'. This was a lightbulb moment for me—I had waited months to hear those words.

The disease (it is just that: 'dis-ease') is not contagious—the sufferers need praise, not criticism. It is a lack of information that leads to the stigma and misunderstanding. Yet it is now a common condition, akin to high blood pressure and back pain. A lack of understanding downplays the severity of the illness. It is an illness as real as any other; it impacts on all areas of life. The stigma, born of ignorance, is still attached, because others can't see the problem. Mum used to say, 'If only I had a broken arm or leg, people could see the problem'.

As with most sufferers, Mum put on a brave face (a mask) to the outside world. She kept much of what she was feeling to herself. She would collapse on the bed the moment she arrived home and increasingly she did not have the energy to prepare the evening meal. Activities that once offered pleasure seemed meaningless, and simple tasks a real struggle. As she reached rock bottom, Mum could no longer even pick flowers from her beloved garden, she could not go to a supermarket: the panic attacks would take over. I think that her bulletproof exterior made it hard (if not impossible) for her to ask for help and support.

It always worsens before it gets better—as the saying goes, 'The night is darkest just before the dawn'. Tuesday, 19 October 2004 is one morning that I will remember for the rest of my life. Finding Mum in bed rolled up in a ball, crying and not wanting to go on living like this anymore. She was taken to hospital by ambulance. The hospital would not admit her because 'mental health is not our problem'. I was told to take her home and a mental health team would assess her in two to three weeks. I have no doubt that had we waited, Mum would not have survived. This woman who we love was acute—needed a wheelchair, could not walk. Our very foundations were rocked. After what was the worst experience that Dad and I have ever had to endure, Mum was admitted to an institute and then a private hospital, where her medication was changed and she underwent intensive therapy.

However, despite all the therapy, Mum says that nothing beats knowing that there are other people out there who truly understand. Advocates for mental health have revealed their personal experiences to increase awareness within the community. These are incredible people who use their profile and experience to help others and throw the spotlight on depression. For Mum, it is finally somebody that really understands—not just the illness, but how to bring about real improvement in quality of life. They help you realise that you are not 'just a sad person', you are not alone, you are not a freak. In our eyes, they are very brave and we admire their honesty and courage.

I am very blessed that Mum was determined to overcome depression. She was not going to let it beat her. Her tenacity and courage won out over this recalcitrant illness. She continues to be an inspiration. I am immensely proud to call her Mum.

The telephone shattered the silence of a hot summer evening in the tropics. I picked up the receiver and the distraught voice of my daughter cried, 'Mum, when am I going to get my brother back?' A few days before, my son Patrick had been admitted to hospital after yet another suicide attempt. My son suffers from bipolar disorder.

As usual, I had taken off to the beach where I hoped that the wind and the waves would relieve some of my pain. I had done this so many times before, and the pattern was always the same. I thought back to the time when I had never heard of bipolar disorder. I thought about Patrick when he was young and then when he was a teenager. To me, he was just a normal kid—hyperactive at times and with the usual growing pains that most teenagers experience. But a few things did appear to be a little different from his mates. He seemed to experience more highs than his friends and these would be followed by extraordinary bouts of deep depression.

For instance, when something interested him, he would plunge feet first into that interest with such tremendous enthusiasm that nothing could stop his feverish activity. He would speak so fast and would be so frantic about his latest interest that nobody could get a word in edgeways. Just listening to him would tire everyone out and leave them drained of energy. In fact, he would exhaust himself until the interest waned and then he would plunge into the depths of despair.

Then, when things were bad, he would find solace in going on wild shopping sprees, spending all his money and begging me to give him more. Of course, he would promise faithfully to pay the money back but he never did. He told me that he felt such a failure. As he got older, this gradually led to alcohol and drug abuse and he began being treated for this.

After one long period of treatment, he met Sophie and I was thrilled when they got married and had two beautiful children. I thought this would settle him down, but the marriage failed and after a number of years there was a divorce. Patrick loved his children dearly and I suspected that he was still in love with Sophie, so this made it hard for him to accept the divorce. He was still being treated for alcohol and drug abuse, and it was at this stage that he was diagnosed with bipolar disorder. From time to time he was hospitalised and had many changes in medication. These times were really bad for everyone as new medication often took several weeks to kick into his system. Sometimes the medication was wrong and the doctors had to start all over again. Also, different doctors had different ways of treating bipolar disorder and this aggravated the situation.

But it enabled me to learn more about Patrick and about this complicated disease. So eventually I listened to what he said and what he believed was good for him personally. At times, he would disappear for days on end and I wouldn't hear from him, but I heard about him from others. They would tell me he had a job, or he was engrossed in some new hobby, or he was meeting new people. But things were never permanent.

When he came home, I tried to pick up the threads and start again. When a new job opportunity came up, I said, 'That's great, Patrick, give it a go!' When that job finished, I said that I was proud of him and then I told him to hang in there until something else turned up. Even with this disease, he retains a great sense of humour and is highly intelligent, artistic and musical. The last bout of depression was particularly bad—he stole my car and wrecked it after a drunken spree. I was so angry that I went down to the beach to walk off my anger as I had done in the past. After that he disappeared and ended up in hospital having tried to suicide again. And that's when my daughter phoned me and desperately wanted to know when she would get her brother back. I had no answer to give her.

266

Young depression

Don't listen to their voice,
Hear instead their silence,
Note how they disengage,

Seeking a cool distance,
Adrift; but not by choice.
What of their eye contact?
There are clues in their eyes.
Masked or slyly downcast,
Some excuse they devise,
To feign vague disinterest.
Do they shy right away,
Indifferent to your joy,
Silent and self-absorbed,
Too aloof to enjoy
Quiet pleasures day to day.
They're detached and remote,
There's no warmth in their smile,
You think them too moody,
You're completely beguiled
And unable to cope.
'It is really your fault',
Why should they compete?
It is their right by birth,
To share the pedestal,
They've erected for you.
Acceptance is their due
Is not their whole enough?
Neither judge nor compare
You should treasure their gifts,
As they love and accept you.
Like a secret black spell,
Their sense of guilt hovers,
They strike wildly at those

They least want to lose,
But they can't dare to tell.
Your love must be proved,
Their worth is the issue,
Be awake to their cry,
If you fail to break through,
They are not truly loved.
There's no easy ingress,
It needs not to be so,
You're outside a locked door,
But how to gain access?
If you love you should know.
Don't accept their withdrawal,
Confide, inquire, persist,
Keep communicating,
Their silence resist,
Until the dam bursts.
Justifying this strife
Begs no explanations,
This is not about you,
No recriminations,
It's just them and their life.
Let them cry themselves out,
And spew forth all their blame,
Let them see how you hurt,
Let the heat of shared shame,
Sear away painful doubts.
Used to having its way
The 'black dog' ever lurks,
It targets its prey; sure

Their self-doubt is a drug,
That so often they'll crave.
Know the rules of the hunt,
The Beast marks its victim
And presumes a welcome.
You must work as a team,
For this fight to be won.

My father had a family tree of black dogs, a genealogy. Small rough-haired mongrels, balls of muscle with the devil's ears, stumpy tails and wry mistrustful eyes. They followed him around, attaching at the ankle when he walked, a quiet pool of darkness whenever he was still. Black shadows that dogged his days, staying loyal to the end.

During my time with depression, I have found that the ones you love the most are the ones you hurt the most. Sometimes, you are so unstable that you say and do things that you would not normally do at other times. Often, you do not even recall what you said or did to your loved one, and, at a later time during conversation, a comment will be made and you can see the sadness in their eyes because of something you have previously said during an episode. Unfortunately, words cannot be taken back once they have been said, but it is so important to remember that the person suffering depression is not always in complete control of their words and actions, and forgiveness has to be given. Forgiveness is one of the most important things that you can give to a depressed person.

Be prepared to just listen. It could literally be the difference between life and death. Far better to sit in silence and hold their hand than to offer a multitude of solutions that they are unable, emotionally and/or mentally, to grasp. Keep it simple. Be calm and encouraging. Empathy, patience, loyalty and trust are the key elements needed to take away the fear, the sadness, the loneliness and the despair. Assure them that they can count on you, and make sure they can!

290

Reading Kafka is a symptom of your illness, not a treatment. It will never, ever cheer you up.

9. Staying on course
Wellbeing strategies

> In riding the storm to normality, we must fight. We are worthy. NEVER, NEVER, NEVER GIVE UP! We can learn, grow and actually benefit from the painful but insightful journey.
>
> 451

In this chapter, people with depression describe what they have found to be useful adjuncts to their medical treatment and of benefit in managing their depression. Reclaiming and nurturing oneself requires effort at multiple levels— physical, social, intellectual, spiritual and personal. It is encouraging to discover that the things that individuals find most effective in minimising the risk of relapse and prolonging periods of wellness are simple, uncomplicated and accessible.

Optimal coping during episodes, and in between episodes, is best achieved through a combination of treatment approaches. Striving to get better, and *stay* better, involves a mix of treatments that is, understandably, person-specific, and dependent on the nature of the depression. However, for all types of depression, there are two ingredients that are indispensable in bolstering recovery and resilience: hope and support.

The narratives we have chosen aim to spark the conviction that stability and a feeling of wellbeing are realistic and achievable, though it is up to each individual to select the strategies that work best for them.

Living with depression is like trying to fit the pieces of a puzzle to make up a picture you have not seen. I slowly came to realise that all the information was useful, but it didn't necessarily apply to me. Other people's stories were very empowering, but I had to be careful not to compare my progress with others. 357

The suggestions are by no means exhaustive and some may appear trite to a person who is currently enveloped in a melancholic fog. There is a danger that such self-help suggestions can make individuals feel worse by pointing up their sense of inadequacy.

Self-help tomes seemed written for others more skilled in the art of living than I was—they only served to batter my already wounded self-esteem when I failed to execute their deceptively simple instructions for a better life. 159

The difference here is that the suggestions in this chapter have been passed on with a generosity of spirit from those who have clawed their way out of their own dark pit. Most writers expressed the hope that sharing what has helped them may lighten the load for others.

Depression's aftermath often leaves behind an enduring sense of vulnerability and sensitivity. However, the safeguards that are put in place during periods of remission are vital to controlling the risk of relapse, and to reducing the impact of any subsequent depressive episode. The key to self-management is taking personal responsibility for the illness, maintaining a commitment to reduce stress and triggers, remaining alert to early warning signs and effecting relevant lifestyle changes.

I have found the best way for me to live with depression is to take action—positive, pleasant, normal, non-violent action. Get up; go for a walk; window shop; read the local newspaper; join the library; learn to use the internet; treat yourself to a chai tea; sleep when exhausted; talk to people if they have time; keep yourself squeaky clean; smell nice; keep cool; don't rush; avoid illegal drugs and alcohol; eat well; study life; watch 'normal' people doing 'normal' things; walk away rather than argue; watch the sunrise; watch the sunset; avoid chemicals; keep away from people using illegal drugs and alcohol; stay in the fresh air as much as possible; soak your feet to relax; ask for help if you need it; get your eyes checked; wear comfortable, proper-fitting footwear; keep away from loud noise; be nice to yourself; be nice to others; eat lots of vegetables; get a hobby; give yourself time; write down what you have to do; ask for information; do something else if you slip into paranoia; smoke away from other people if you haven't quit; wear sunglasses; change TV channels if something upsets you; listen to the police; don't buy it if you can't afford it; wander around a museum; get organised; have a café latte and browse through the café's magazines; make notes on your observations; take an interest in the world around you; watch documentaries; don't over-spice your food; read a book at the library; keep your scalp clean; ignore other people's rudeness; save to go to the movies to escape; wear cotton clothing; keep your room clean; join the Women's Movement; join the Men's Movement; vote; don't interrupt working people; cross at the lights; avoid repetitive music; stop doors banging; wash the curtains; join Greenpeace; learn something new every day; buy new socks; use sunscreen; join in your country's celebrations; don't make a mess to come back to; phone the relevant complaint line if you have a genuine complaint; go to the student theatre; enjoy Christmas; do a MENSA test; laughter is still the best medicine; avoid violent people; if your head hurts, stop and rest; don't wear tight clothing; if you feel clammy have a bird bath; try to look and think before you speak; rest your eyes; relax your jaw; have a break every two hours; massage your feet; save for a professional haircut; check prices on your receipts; look for a bargain; stay alert; stand your ground in a queue; take a ferry trip; walk in the shade; learn about the things that frighten you; don't try and memorise everything; be polite; wash your face; keep calm; drink water; run away if you're attacked; cut out the sugar; double-check the bus timetables; keep your toenails short; sleep at night; play Patience; say so when you don't understand; keep an eye on your bank account; if you don't want it don't buy it; try your luck—buy a lottery ticket; buy new underwear; try herbal teas; try a two-hour slow walk on a cool day; keep a written record of your life; check out your family tree; go to the doctor every year; walk in the moonlight; keep the TV volume low; wear clean clothes every day; give yourself a manicure; write names, addresses and phone numbers in an address book; read what you're signing; buy a new pillow every six months; clean up the cooking smells straightaway; recycle; keep the cobwebs away; don't fight sleep; check the weather reports; watch the birds; enter competitions; put your feet up; ignore bullies; carry a water bottle; try a vegetarian meal; avoid loud people; check your bank statements; get a skin cancer check; always carry change for the bus; use a pumice stone; read all the junk mail; wash your glasses; avoid steps if it hurts; put your dirty laundry in a zip-up bag; be nice to your grandmother; dust with a damp cloth often; wear a cool hat; learn to type; try yoghurt; wash your sheets more often; try and plan your days; wash your eyes; sharpen your pencils; use a cooler bag for shopping; change your deodorant; learn about food; wash your purse or wallet; read all the community centres' brochures; drink de-caf; use fresh herbs; use a facial scrub; splash around in the rock pool; do a crossword puzzle. Try and do SOMETHING every day and increase it until you can think more clearly.

Stop thinking. Stop over-thinking and dwelling and becoming overwhelmed and panicked and exhausted. Enough! I listened to my own negative feedback for many, many years and I had had enough.

That was the first step: absolute and dogged determination not to let this disease ruin any more of my life. As I have discovered, there is so much more to life. Sources of inspiration provide me with a perspective that depression represses.

Some days it is easier to control than other days. On the bad days, and these are few now, I let go. I feel too stuck, too over-whelmed to focus on anything other than negative memories, insecurities and hopelessness. I give up fighting it and relax. I take the day off work, skip social functions and ignore obligations. I call it my 'mental health day' and, ironically, I feel better for allowing myself to feel depressed.

To wake in the morning feeling vulnerable and blind as a baby mole, and then allow myself to work through it so that by evening I am not just happy but joyous and hopeful; this is a gigantic, monumental feat. I am a slayer of dragons, an alchemist turning base metals to gold, a magician, a worker of miracles. And yet, for all that, it is a very silent victory, for all I may have done is get up, go to an art gallery then go home and read a book. But anyone who knows depression knows this can be near impossible.

A day such as this, where I have broken the shackles of negativity, even for a few hours, will lead to other more positive days. It is a skill that can be practised and improved. As good days become more frequent, motivation hangs around long enough to put ideas into action. And then self-esteem flowers.

For me, overcoming depression means learning to focus outside yourself, and moving forward from pain and mistakes of the past. From that first time you succeed in feeling better on your own, and relying only on yourself, you gain a skill. You practise the skill so that eventually you know how to find new friendships, hobbies, a sense of community. It leads to further education, and healthy relationships with partners and families.

As I get better, I watch my positivity spread. It leaps from person to person and picks them up on an upward spiral. I laugh and enjoy the happiness of others. In getting better and being content, I give something back to the society that has put up with me absorbing only myself. I can now touch the lives of others. I never thought I would say these things seven years ago!

I don't know if I'll ever be completely rid of depression. But I no longer feel unlucky or hard done by. Because when my head is above the water, life's little problems seem trivial and comparatively easy to cope with.

Emotionally detach yourself from too close a bond with the highs and lows of life. Placidly accept failure with a shrug of the shoulders. Any means that can reduce focus on the self and increase it on the broader universe is welcome. Discover how to tame the tiger of the mind—this presents a path to eternal peace. Have one, single achievement every day; no matter how small, it's a start.

In the case of my black dog, exercise was a key factor. Everyone had told me that being active would help, but at first his sheer size made it almost impossible. I'd think about going for a run, but there he was, blocking the door, his great paws threatening to knock me down every time I tried to get the leash around his throat. It was easier just to stay on the couch. One day though I got up early and took him by surprise—we were out of the house and into the park before he'd properly woken up. The funny thing was though, that once we were there, I'm sure he enjoyed it. Endorphins, I'm told, are chemicals released during exercise that act as a natural form of antidepressant. Since then I've tried swimming, dancing, cycling and always the daily walk. My black dog usually comes with me, but I swear that by the time we finish, he never looks as big as he did at the start.

Along with exercise, grooming is also important. By and large, black dogs are ugly creatures—all melancholy eyes and lacklustre coats. Take the trouble to dress yours up a bit though and you'll be surprised at the difference. A quick brush or a new collar may feel like a bit too much effort at times, but have a look at the effect on your dog. Isn't he picking up his feet a bit more? Sniffing the lamp posts with renewed interest? And note how others are noticing, and in turn find your beast less frightening, more approachable. That makes him feel better too. It's only a little thing, but looking good can advance the transformation to feeling good.

Then there's diet. To better manage your black dog, you should be watching what he eats: ideally, the sort of balanced diet they're always banging on about in the dog food commercials. In other words, make sure your black dog's breakfast isn't a dog's dinner. And watch out for chicken bones.

And, of course, no obedience training can be complete without appropriate discipline. Sure, it would be easier just to let him have his way, but let's remember who's the master here. Do you really want to listen to him howl all night, or have him scare all your friends away? Discipline is about working through the hard yards every day—getting out of bed; making sure you eat enough; doing some exercise; brushing your teeth; and going out even when it doesn't feel as if any progress is being made. It is—even if only by the simple act of not giving in.

And, above all, don't punish yourself. You didn't ask for the black dog, but it's not your fault he's there either. Chances are he just followed you home.

Just remember that training takes time and effort. Every black dog is different, and, of course, they all have their days. It's hard to turn a pug into a poodle, and it has to be said that success *isn't* guaranteed. But that doesn't mean you shouldn't try. There are bound to be times when you will feel you're fighting a losing battle, and often that's when you need to get others involved. Some people like to call in the professionals, the black dog experts, if you will. When you're stuck, these people will know what to try next or can make sure you're headed in the right direction. There are rarely quick fixes, and you'll have to commit yourself to staying the course. But if you do, you might just find that after a while your black dog is significantly more obedient or has even skulked off altogether.

Others might simply want to call on a friend or two. Black dogs are exhausting—sometimes you just need someone else to help you hold the leash for a while, or even follow behind with a pooper scooper. Friends can help by listening, talking, reassuring, by sticking by you and getting you involved in other non-canine activities. It's hard to do this entirely by yourself—in most cases it really does help to see a man (or woman) about a dog.

And that's about it. Nothing too magical, nothing miraculous, but the black dog can be brought to heel by a combination of things. Regular exercise for a start, good grooming, the right diet (and make sure you stay away from the hair of the dog!). Try to get plenty of rest—let sleeping dogs lie—and don't be too hard on yourself. Find someone you can talk to, be that a professional or a friend, someone who acknowledges your black dog and knows how to handle him. The black dog will never be man's best friend, but, with a bit of work and help, with any luck you will eventually be able to put your own dog days behind you.

407

I have learnt to spot the warning signs and now act as soon as possible to nip it in the bud, although there seems to be an element of denial with me, which often prevents me intervening as early as I should. Once depression starts, it grabs hold of me with an unrelenting grasp like the iron jaws of a steel cutter.

So I have decided that prevention is far preferable to cure.

Some of the tricks I use to deal with the unwanted, negative thoughts and messages mimic those I employ to control all those unwanted emails and spam. I delete them from my mind and picture the computer icon emptying them into the delete box. Better still, I try to use my own internal spam filter to get rid of those wicked vibes before they have the audacity to enter my psyche.

Survival guide for the severely depressed

Step 1: Wage war. Have faith that the war you wage will win back your life. Stand up and fight. You will lose some battles and sometimes be taken prisoner, but whatever it is that makes your heart beat, whatever keeps your lungs inhaling, is the same primal force that will have you winning in the end. Wage war does not mean soldier on. What you need to win is the strength to surrender and seek help, the strength to admit weakness.

Step 2: Go mad. Just as visually impaired people are blind and hearing-impaired people are deaf, depressed people are mad. No amount of politically correct avoidance language can alter this. Take possession of your madness, after all, you own it. Realise its tragedy and its sadness but also understand how ridiculous and perversely funny it is, and laugh at it. Take heart.

History is full of honourable people, worthy of great admiration, who were stark raving mad.

When you are depressed, there are choices you can make that will eventually set you free.

292

I have experienced at least six episodes of depression, each one becoming more severe. The thought of having another episode still fills me with fear. And yet my life is good—I have an under-standing partner and two great children, a good job, reasonable health, good friends, enough money and, significantly, plans for the future.

Recognising depression, and most importantly accepting it, has been crucial for me to be able to live successfully with it. This sounds so obvious, but, for me and others, this is hard to do because of the social stigma involved and a great sense of personal failure. Recognising the condition in the early stages can be hard because of the usually insidious nature of the illness.

What I have found most useful in early detection is being aware and knowing my first signs, which are mostly physical. My body feels trapped in a slow-motion movie sequence and I begin to wake in the early hours of the morning. The longer this goes on, the more severe the depression gets and the more pervasive. Each time it happens, I go through the same difficult process of trying to fight it and not wanting to accept that it is back again.

I have found that being able to say 'I suffer from depression', even to myself, has a better effect on the way I view myself than saying 'I am depressed'. By naming depression it takes on an identity outside of me and allows me to separate myself from the illness. Doing this allows me to acknowledge the symptoms of depression, knowing they are symptoms of an illness not my whole self. After all, I don't say I am a broken arm, or I am a tumour, or I am the flu, or I am glandular fever, or I am a toothache. I know that these conditions affect part of myself, not my whole self.

Unfortunately, with depression, there is a tendency to identify oneself with the illness because it affects one's thought processes and one's perspective, one's way of looking at oneself and the world. Once I am able to name the depression, it is easier (but still not easy) to accept a task-oriented approach to addressing the symptoms.

Getting to this stage is difficult for me and talking with an understanding, non-judgemental person who is empathic and supportive and directive when I need direction is important for me. My partner and my GP have been wise and caring, allowing me the space to recognise what is happening without taking control. Having someone who understands this process and is patient enough to allow you to talk it through is invaluable.

Through practising meditation I have been able to combat the onset of stress and restlessness, slow my breathing as a defence mechanism against fears and feelings of vulnerability, and lower my blood pressure. It has given me a sense of inner calm and stability. It has increased my confidence and self-esteem, and has given me invaluable insights into the factors which contribute to a sense of joy, optimism and gratitude in life.

I have begun to understand that my sense of self-worth is not dependent on how other people see or react to me.

A related practice I have found to be successful in fighting off my depression and morbid self-absorption has been the pursuit of gratifications, which produce a sense of 'flow', or total immersion, and mental clarity. I have begun a journal in which I record these gratifications, whether it is the stimulating conversation I had with a friend, the book I read that revealed to me new insights, or a meal I cooked that required skill and stretched my culinary ability. The feelings of satisfaction and sharing from engaging in such activities have contributed to my ongoing wellbeing and sense of self-worth and engagement with life.

While I have cautiously rekindled the flames of old friendships, I also spend time alone, walking in the countryside or along the beach or river with my dog, or going back to what I have done well in the past: writing, photography and painting. Slowly, I have reconnected with my creative self. I have heeded the wise counsel of Australian poet, Peter Bakowski:

> look . . .
> for the virtue within yourself
> what you have done, what you have mastered,
> no matter how small the arena,
> and what it is that you must do
> now.
> (*In the Human Heart,* 1995, p. 69)

When the black dog is your companion, the *last* thing you may want is another self-help book or guide telling you how to live with it! Although well-meaning and informative, they can sound hollow when you are in the depths of despair. Full of clichés and advice, they can sometimes make you feel even worse. Depression is a unique experience, and each person has their own individual journey through it. When you are feeling down, it can feel like you are the only person who has ever felt so bad—and that nothing on earth will help you.

I can only share my own experience and reassure you, *it will pass.* It may linger but it will eventually lift. Just as it gradually appeared with no realisation that you were getting depressed, one day the black dog will no longer be at your feet and you will wonder where he has gone. In the meantime, making this phase of life tolerable, and speeding up your progress through it, is crucial. It is important to recognise that you are not alone. Many people have experienced depression and it is not something to feel ashamed of or guilty about.

345

I would like to say that reading about depression is important. However, support is perhaps right up the top for me, while looking after your health physically, spiritually and emotionally is also crucial. Talking with people with the same type of illness, and just people in general, is good. Isolation is not so good, but we all need some of it to have a good cry or somehow get these demons out.

I have worked hard to get where I am and I still have a way to go. I can feel it. I am not cured. I don't think there is a cure, just manageability. Everybody is different but I am coping better and I'm not being so secretive about my depression.

218

Congratulations on becoming the owner of your very own black dog. Most people who own black dogs never intended to. The black dog was just sitting by their bed one day when they woke up. Or he had been lurking at the back door for a while and finally moved in. And most black dog owners agree they don't really have time for it. The black dog seems to get in the way of all the things that are beautiful and fun in life.

The black dog is quite different from the blue dog, although they are related. The blue dog sometimes moves in when you are grieving, under great stress, going through a break-up or making difficult changes in your life. He makes you feel a little, well, blue. The blue dog can be difficult to manage, but he's not likely to move into your house for good and may only stay a few weeks.

But the black dog . . . Well, sometimes it feels as if the black dog owns you—and not the other way around. If you've never owned a black dog before, and are wondering what to do with him, this guide is for you. Most owners agree: the brute needs looking after, and you need some strategies to help you live with it.

Give the dog space, but not too much: Respecting the space the black dog needs is important. You will not feel like a party animal with a black dog clinging to your back. So take time out and be alone if that is what you need to do.

But the black dog is a solitary creature. He'd like it to be just the two of you forever. Even though that's what the black dog is craving, too much time alone might not be the best thing for you right now.

So you need to find a way to stay connected. By all means, screen your calls—but try to return one each day. Or, if talking seems too hard, email or text just one of the people who love you. They are still there. It's very important that you keep talking to people. Dogs—and black dogs particularly—aren't really good conversationalists.

But when you don't want to talk to anyone, don't beat yourself up over it. Wander around a shopping mall or go to a movie. Walk to a cafe and drink good coffee in the sun. Stay in the world, even if only for a little while.

Feed the black dog: Owning a black dog can play havoc with your eating habits. Sometimes he won't want to eat and food holds no appeal. Eat simply and regularly, even if you can only face soup and toast. Sometimes he won't want to stop eating and could happily devour the entire freezer section of the local supermarket. At these times, eat well and concentrate on fruit and vegetables.

A word of warning—black dogs and alcohol don't mix. Alcohol is a depressant, which can make the black dog even meaner. Have you ever seen a drunken Doberman? Alcohol doesn't mix with prescription medications either, so avoid alcohol, and avoid other drugs too. Your body and mind are coping with enough already.

Remember that the soul also needs to be fed. Do things that comfort and nourish you. Read—but avoid beauty magazines and self-help books. Start a journal. Meditate. Listen to music. Get a massage. Swim in the ocean. Get enough sleep. Watch a comedy and laugh if you can. Try to get out of the house at least once a day. Do one of these things every day, even if the black dog doesn't want to.

Exercise the black dog: A little gentle exercise is so good for the black dog. It releases chemicals in your body which can ease depression. But the black dog loves bed. He'd like you to stay there all day. Bargaining may be the only option: make an agreement with the black dog that if you can take him round the block, he can curl up in bed afterwards. Sometimes, he won't even want to go back to bed after you've been out. And if you miss a day, be gentle with yourself. Try again tomorrow. Aim for a little exercise every day. Anything is better than nothing.

When the black dog won't listen: Sometimes, despite your best efforts, the black dog will not stay on his lead. He will not sit or stay, and he certainly won't heel. These are the times when you literally can't get out of bed. Can't be bothered showering. Can't stop crying. Can't see the point in carrying on.

Your black dog needs immediate remedial obedience training. Take him to see your doctor. Your GP might suggest trying medication to help tame it. Antidepressants are very effective for many people. Don't be alarmed at the thought of taking medication. If you had a heart condition, you wouldn't hesitate to take the medicine your doctor prescribed. You have a medical condition, just like many other people. Your doctor might also suggest you see a counsellor, psychotherapist, psychologist or a psychiatrist. Your doctor and other health professionals are your allies and will work with you to get the black dog back under control.

You are not your black dog: Sometimes it feels like all you are is the black dog. It feels like there is nothing else. But that's not the case. You are also the clever, loving, beautiful, successful person everyone says you are. It can just be very hard to see it when the black dog casts its shadow.

If you can, keep some perspective—however small it may be.

Remember, you didn't always feel like this. You won't always feel like this. You are not alone.

When the black dog sleeps: Sometimes the black dog sleeps or even, bless him, goes into hibernation. One morning you might wake up to find the black dog isn't at the end of your bed. He's not under it, and he's not waiting in the kitchen either. Breathe in. The air feels lighter and smells sweeter. Stretch. Use this time to enjoy some space from the black dog. See the friends you have missed. See movies or shows. Get back to the gym, or start painting again. Tidy up the house.

Good luck . . . The black dog can bring with him the darkest hours in your life. But, sometimes, knowing the darkest hours helps you appreciate the brighter days. You can take pleasure in the smallest things—a friendly smile on the train, the blossom trees in spring, a friend's good news.

And each time the black dog pays you a visit, you get better at anticipating and managing him. You learn to recognise him as he pads down the hallway towards you. He becomes a little less scary the more time you spend with him, until he becomes, if not a friend, a familiar companion. And since you've survived his visits before, you know that you can get through them again.

The black dog can teach you to be gentle with yourself, and to take care of yourself. You learn to encourage and be kind to yourself. You can learn to listen to not only the black dog, but the rest of you that is still there underneath the dog.

Owning a black dog can also teach you to be more compassionate towards others—to recognise others who might have this beast as well. Maybe, one day, you might even be able to help them learn how to live with their own black dogs.

I have found that the best way to help myself, when I am feeling able to do things, is to set some routines in place. I have a book (which no-one else is allowed to see) and in it I wrote a list of twenty things that I like to do. They did not have to cost money, but some of them did. I like to watch rain falling on a pool, I like to look at the stars at night, I like to watch the sun set. I like to feel invisible sometimes, sit in a very busy place, like a large shopping centre, and watch people who are usually in a big hurry to get somewhere. It can be very important to realise that there are other people around, *and* watching them shop or getting their lunch or running jobs in their lunch hour takes away your feeling of isolation. Sometimes I go to the movies on my own, which I found a really daunting task the first time, but it does get easier the more times you do it. You can sit and fill in some of your day in the darkness of the cinema and let your emotions flow and no-one knows.

I have a box in which I keep every card or letter that is given to me. I keep this box within easy access, and when I have a day when I feel that no-one loves me, or that I am unworthy, I open this box and read what is written on the cards. It is a simple reminder to myself that I have people around me that care for me and have faith in me. It is an encouragement to myself when I am low. It is such a simple thing, but it can be so helpful when I am low and by myself.

I ask myself questions and write the answers in my book. Questions like, 'If I was not suffering depression, what would I be doing?' or 'If I was in perfect health, what would I want to be doing?' or 'If I could do anything I wanted, what would I do?' or 'If I could be anyone, who would I be and why?' I find when I start to write, I get fully involved with what I am doing. It makes me think about ways that I can improve my life and what I have to do to make these things happen. In this book I also write anything that is important to me. It may be something that someone has said to me, a quote I have read or just something that I feel I need to express for myself. When I am having a bad day, I read through this book and it helps me put perspective back into my life.

520

For me, prayer was a major factor in restoring balance in my life. God became for me, as T.S. Eliot put it so well, my 'still point of the turning world' (Eliot, 1995, p. 5). When the world around me seems unfriendly, unstable and unsupportive, I know that God is there and this knowledge helps me to regain and retain my balance. My ability to pray to God, to engage in a personal relationship where I can be truly open, has been indescribably important.

I know from experience that attacks of depression can occur at any time, no matter how well I feel just now, and to withstand these attacks I need my armour. I don't have to pull myself together—the path-to-health process will instead be developed in conjunction with those who love me (and whom I love), those who laugh with me, those who use their specialist skills to support me, and the God with whom I speak continuously. This knowledge gives me great peace.

187

I once heard depression described as the 'common cold' of the mind. Anyone, anytime, anywhere can succumb to it. Unfortunately, you can't remove the risk factor altogether, any more than you can eliminate the possibility of catching a cold. However, you can minimise the effects and hopefully ensure a speedier recovery if ever you do get bitten by the black dog.

There is one tonic that I would highly recommend: a good dose of humour. Granted, it's hard to find something to laugh about when you feel like your world is caving in around you. There is definitely nothing funny about that.

I have a 'happy folder' full of borrowed humour, and I keep it close by. It is filled with amusing anecdotes and humorous tidbits, along with comical clippings from newspapers, calendars or books. It also contains cards and letters brimming with words of encouragement, along with inspiring magazine articles about ordinary people overcoming extraordinary odds. There are also pictures of captivating beauty that remove me far from the ugliness and pain of my real world. I'd rather be lost in a world of imagination for a few brief hours then succumb to the overwhelming sadness that can trap me in the grip of despair for weeks at a time.

Learn to self-distract rather than self-destruct. Listening to music, reading, or writing in a journal can be very helpful. Jigsaw puzzles can be very therapeutic and a great way to distract your attention away from those disquieting thoughts. Just like a jigsaw puzzle comes together one piece at a time, it's a good reminder that we should tackle our problems one at a time. We may feel fragmented inside, but, like that puzzle, when viewed on the whole, it reveals a beautiful picture. We need to remember that family and friends see the whole picture. They see us, not our illness.

No truer saying is, 'You cannot control the direction of the wind, but you can adjust your sails'. Our own attitude can help or hinder good mental health. Sometimes, we can feel like our life is 'missing' something. But would a doughnut really taste any better without the hole in the middle? Always remember that we have something to be thankful for. Try to never overlook life's little joys while searching for the bigger ones. A cinnamon doughnut can be just as filling as a chocolate eclair!

The sayings 'A problem shared is a problem halved' and 'There is strength in numbers' are very true. You should never be ashamed of your illness. The more people you have in your network of support, the better. Hiding depression only adds to the frustration, pain and anxiety that it brings. That overwhelming sense of loneliness . . . there are no words to describe that. This is not an illness you can or should always try to fight on your own. Sometimes you have to admit that you need help.

People in physical pain are sometimes advised not to fight it but embrace it instead and, amazingly enough, it does work. Some days the best way to fight the black dog is to give it a great big bear hug. Why allow your illness to control your life? Take control of your illness instead. The choice is yours, and even that is empowerment.

290

Own it. Accept it. Educate yourself. Read autobiographies. Talk to your GP. Ask questions and ask for help. Talk about how you feel. Keep busy and active. Find a craft. Join a club. Do crosswords. Meditate. Be kind to yourself. Have an open mind to advice. Pursue challenges. Just don't do nothing.

39

When I sense the onset of a low period, I no longer try to pretend it isn't happening because, if I do, I just end up getting more distressed, more anxious, spiralling ever downwards, and it takes me a longer time to recover. Whereas once I would have struggled with the 'pull your chin up' mode of thinking, and tried to avoid the low by keeping extra busy, I now have a different strategy. I allow myself to openly wallow for a day or two: to cry, to brood, to dwell repeatedly on my failings, to see nothing good in anyone, or the world in general. And then there comes a point where I am so wrung out and so low that I have only one way to go, and that has to be up.

However, I still treat myself gently for the next few days, exactly the same as if I were recovering from a physical illness like the flu, and I take certain steps to help me along the way. While it is not always possible to avoid the frenetic pace of modern life, I go *slow* on as many levels as possible. I make a conscious effort not to over-analyse things (not easy, but with practice one can do it). Avoiding as much media as I can certainly helps—especially news reports on TV, radio or internet. I also avoid reading magazines that feed off our dissatisfaction with ourselves in their obsession with body image, financial success or enviable lifestyles. I take it easy with caffeine and alcohol, and I eat lightly (although a small amount of chocolate never hurts). I do not push myself to do anything that is not essential, or give in to any 'should' or 'ought to' commands lurking in my mind. I enjoy simple pleasures—reading, pottering in the garden, listening to relaxing music. It follows that when doing any exercise, anything that is fast, competitive or punishing is out. Surprisingly, insomnia tends to be less of a problem when one is on a 'go slow'.

After a few days of this regime, I usually find that I switch to a better frame of mind and I can more easily move up a couple of notches into a faster pace of life and not feel stressed or worried. Throughout my recovery process, I also make sure I always find plenty to laugh at—including myself.

156

For me, fighting depression is a balance between the mind, body and spirit.

The mind: Strategies for distracting my mind from the bad thoughts, reading, TV, DVDs, listening to music, joining up with a community mental health group, changing my negative thoughts to positive thoughts, cognitive behavioural therapy and finding the right medication.

The body: Looking after my physical health, eating and sleeping well, walking every day, dealing with my stress levels, using the Mental Health Association's '10 Steps to Stress Less' (I have a card on my board at work, I actually read it and do it), call a friend and have lunch, make time for myself to do things that I enjoy. Recently I have been using float tanks and massage, and I find these very good for stress and anxiety.

The spirit: Having a good spiritual life, being with nature, and having a religious life. My spiritual journey towards recovery from depression began when I was hiking with a friend. I came face-to-face with the complete beauty of the mountains for the first time. I realised this was what my spirit had been craving for most of my life. It stirred me to writing some poetry, sitting by a river in the sun.

Relationships: Having good relationships combines all the above. Peer support was important in my recovery. Giving and receiving love from a partner, my son and friends.

Recovery: Slowly I began on my road to recovery. I told my psychiatrist I needed to talk to other people who had a mental illness. He referred me to a rehabilitation program. I worked hard on this program for three years. I was determined to get well and be a good mother for my son—this was my motivation to stick to my program, which is very hard to do when you are depressed.

Motivation: I had a lot of struggles with lack of motivation— doing the dishes and housework was very difficult for me. I managed to keep us clothed and fed, but it was a major battle. My psychiatrist said he wished he could give me a pill for lack of motivation, but there wasn't one. However, I learnt a good strategy to help me with this from a friend, who said, 'When you are about to do the dishes, say to yourself, "I will do this for ten minutes"'. Once I started, I could finish the job; I still find this works for me after ten years.

Advocacy: I started to get involved with many committees and my local Area Consumer Network. I did a consumer education course and heard other consumers speak. They spoke about power. I had always been a union person. I understood that consumers need to work together for change to happen. They spoke about advocacy, self-advocacy and systems advocacy. They spoke about training consumers to work in the hospital wards and the community, and told us they get paid. I was very impressed with this. I learnt I could do what I wanted to do and get paid. I had finally found the career I wanted.

My goal was to get a life, to have good relationships with my partner, family and friends, a career that I was passionate about, and a good spiritual life. I learnt it is important for recovery to have meaningful work.

I gradually explored reasons that may have contributed to my depression, and looked at addressing these issues.

I identified my negative thinking patterns. For me, two main thoughts that I struggled with were the need to keep others happy and the need to be liked by everyone.

I frequently walked outdoors in the fresh air. At times, this is probably the only thing that gave me any sense of hope.

I made myself sit and just *be* in the moment. I still constantly need to remind myself to do this. I was extremely agitated in my blackest dog days. I would constantly be thinking ahead of myself, or rehashing past events in my mind.

I attended a mindfulness course, and commenced practising meditation.

I practised eating slowly, sitting down to eat, and thinking about each mouthful. When I do this, I now taste again. When I was unwell, food had no taste. Therefore I got no enjoyment out of meals, and this, of course, exacerbated my feeling of 'what's the point of life anyway?'.

I started trying to keep to my paid work hours ONLY. I used to routinely work anywhere from three to fifteen hours per week unpaid.

I'm slowly getting myself into the habit of not thinking about work stuff in home time—this still requires ongoing practice!

I resumed doing hobbies that I'd enjoyed in the past. For me, this included arts and crafts, playing a team sport, gardening and writing poetry. I started reading for leisure again: initially, small articles when I had poor concentration, but later whole books. It took quite some time to find pleasure in these hobbies again.

I'd take two steps forward and one step back—and remind myself that this was OK.

I'd get out in the sunshine as often as I could. I felt blacker in winter than in summer.

I started to re-examine my values, and realised life isn't a race, but a process.

I returned to simple living, trying to eat healthier—more fruit, vegetables and fish, and less processed, fatty foods.

If I was tired, I'd try to have a nap, as long as it wasn't likely to affect my night-sleeping patterns.

I read, as much as I could lay my hands on, about experiences of others with depression, how they coped and what they'd noticed. I shared these insights with family and friends. The reading made it all seem real, and helped me to realise I wasn't alone, that others had gotten through this before.

I allowed myself to believe that I have an illness, that I'm not making this up, and that the depression is no less valid than any other (physical) illness.

I gradually told some friends, family members and a couple of close work colleagues. I was careful about who I chose though, only picking those who I was 100 per cent certain would support me, and respect my confidentiality.

I began attending social situations again, starting with brief and small gatherings initially, before gradually building up.

I increasingly turned off the TV, with its depressing news stories.

I took a slightly extended break off work, and allowed myself to get away totally.

I looked tentatively to the future, and set some medium-term goals.

I identified my personal sources of hope, and my relapse-prevention strategies, which included all of the above.

I know deep inside that I want more than anything to avoid EVER feeling depressed again. I realise that to do this I need to recognise the 'grey dog' early, and I need to be proactive at taking preventative steps.

My life is now pastel, with some bits of grey, and the occasional blackness. It also has the occasional rainbow! It has taken a lot of work to get to this point, mainly because there is no one, easy solution. But by using the above strategies, I've found hope for the future.

I cannot tell you how to live with the black dog. I can only tell you how I have learnt to live with him. When in his company, do not drink yourself into a stupor, even under the guise of a friendly night out with friends. The dog's smell may not bother you so much when you are blind drunk; you may even find that you are senselessly happy. But when your senses return the next day or a week later—if that is when you choose to sober up—you will smell the stench of wet fur and doggie breath and you will not be able to escape it. Be careful! You will go deeper down into the hole you are digging for yourself, and even those who love you will not be able to reach you down there.

Only take drugs prescribed by your physician and even then, take them sensibly. I have spent weeks numbed by marijuana, forgetting to wash my hair and seeing the world only in shades of grey. It was only effective for a short while. Try not to take mind-numbing drugs. I know it is hard, but try.

It is the black dog's intention to encourage you into solitude. Do not let him. Open your curtains every morning so that you may see out into the world and let the world see into you—there is nothing to be ashamed of in there. It may be easier to withdraw into yourself but this is not a journey that can be made on your own. It is an expedition that demands trusty companions.

Seek out a trusted friend; seek out a trusted therapist. Both are important. Pay your therapist promptly; he or she will help you in ways that deserve to be rewarded. If you find that you do not like your therapist, do not leave immediately; give them some time. Consider that it is perhaps not the therapist who you do not like, but the piercing honesty with which they hit the buttons of your heart. A good friend will help in other ways, but do not phone too often in the middle of the night—even the most patient friends have their limits. Do not be ashamed to ask for help; you will know soon enough which of your friends and family can handle the pressure.

Try to get up with a purpose every morning, even if that purpose may only be to brush your teeth. The black dog may sneer at your effort to maintain a sense of routine, but at least you will not be plagued by his bad breath. If you want to cry, do so on the floor—it will ground you. If you have been crying for the whole day, have a shower, drink some chocolate milk and put yourself to bed, but don't forget to brush your teeth. Simple daily rituals like this may be the only thing between you and a life abandoned to the black dog.

Do not sleep for more than ten hours every day and do not put yourself to bed until after eight in the evening—once again, the normalcies of daily life will keep you sane. If you cannot sleep, try meditation or music or chocolate milk. As a last resort, consider sleeping pills because a bad night's rest will rub salt in the wound of anxious thoughts. Beware though, the black dog bites back once the effects of any drug have worn off.

Put down the baseball bat when you make a mistake. Don't beat yourself up. Remember that mistakes happen, and it is very likely that the situation is not nearly as serious as you perceive it to be. The black dog paints almost everything in the colours of pessimism and those of us who live under his spell are prone to negative thoughts that border on the extreme.

Surround yourself with people who make you feel good, even if that means getting rid of friends and lovers that have been making you feel bad for years. You cannot so easily get rid of family. Find other ways to deal with them.

Let go of your anger; it is the only way to heal yourself. It could take years to do this, but one day you may look into yourself and find that the anger is no longer there; it has dissolved like sugar in water. This is one of the most wonderful feelings in the world; you will feel as light as a helium balloon set afloat in a clear blue sky.

Clean your house once a week and do not clutter it up with 'stuff' you do not need. 'Stuff' can be dangerous. Some people acquire 'stuff' to hide the black dog, but, really, he is too big to hide.

Clean your emotional wounds. You will need to scrape the pus out of those deep psychological scratches and cuts that have been seeping for years. Nothing will heal properly until you dig out all the muck. It is a painful process but it is the only way to stop the festering thoughts. You may scar, but you will remember these scars as personal triumphs and wear them as trophies.

Keep hope and remember that you were once happy and whole. You can put yourself back together bit by bit, and, who knows, the end product may be better than the one with which you began.

Keep hope! I know I do.

This is my life. It could be better, but it could be a hell of a lot worse. And in my mother's words: 'At least you're leading an interesting life.'

10. The view from the top
Some positives

To grow to flower, even if it's a rocky place.

Some of the bleakness, pain and isolation of depression—humankind's 'black plague of the soul'—has been captured in these pages. However, the following accounts highlight the fact that many people who have been afflicted with depression come through their episodes with positives to recount.

It is a fact that people can lose many things to depression. In the fight for sanity and peace, an individual can be brought to their knees, forced to strip their lives down to the barest elements, questioning values, goals and truths once held dear in order to combat the pain. However, it is clear from these stories that despite the suffering there are some gains in living with, and mastering, one's black dog.

Many writers acknowledged that knowing pain also means you have the opportunity to experience joy. Some individuals re-evaluate their goals, are kinder to themselves, change their priorities, learn to relax, discover new friends and hobbies, seek out their ultimate life purpose, get rid of negative people and influences, become more assertive, find their own peace, and are brought closer to family and friends. Some experience a spiritual awakening, while some are inspired to help others and fight the stigma of mental illness. Most experience a growth of compassion, empathy and gratitude that enriches their lives.

After all, some precious gems are black too. When the depression lifts and the fog recedes, when colours begin to sparkle again, people often feel a renewed self-respect, an intense appreciation for life and pleasure and a new capacity for joy. So, in the words of one writer, we hope this chapter helps you 'turn on a lightbulb or two' (290).

The shapes of light

The half-light settles, like a swan.
Then sometimes sweetly on the tongue,
Like first love tasted by the young,
The shadows move and fall away;
As redemption lingers with the day.
The light becomes a shawl of lace,
Full of beauty, depth and grace,
And once where only demons stood,
There is a pathway through the wood.
We don't see things as they are,
We see them lit by our own bright star.

You have to want to get out of there. I personally will never leave my happiness to the fate of chance and luck. You need to seek out and find any source of inspiration that you can—if you see a tiny glimmer of hope, swim towards it. Where there's a will, there's a way. You will also need a map, a plan, a clear idea to help you chart your course in life to avoid becoming wrecked upon the rocks of sorrow once again.

To truly know black is to truly know white. You will be able to fully and completely understand and grasp just how pure and beautiful life truly is and can be; you can taste the flavour of life with such joy it can bring tears to your eyes; you can find moments of joy everywhere—gain happiness from simple pleasures.

402

While there is nothing inspiring about the experience of depression, some become attuned to the small gifts their suffering brings. They allow, to some extent, the darkness to guide them. Like a windmill catches a fierce breeze to power a house, or gutters collect rainwater from the storm for drinking, some sufferers find comfort in channelling the darkness into the creative, or forging avenues that help other sufferers.

471

You could give up, but you won't, because as well as having a bio-chemical imbalance in your brain, you also have a remarkable resilience in your soul . . . and four magic words that keep you going—This too will pass. It might not be this afternoon, or tomorrow, or next week, but this depression WILL pass and you WILL survive it.

183

When the depression finally lifted, I felt a new sense of self. It was a different me that emerged from the cocoon of darkness. It took time to get there, and it wasn't easy. But I was ultimately enriched from the experience. I learnt a new lifestyle that is a great foundation for the rest of my life—good times and bad. I learnt about my inner strength and resilience, and about how simple things in life can sometimes be the most powerful.

Be gentle with yourself, and trust that this process will leave you with some positive outcomes such as greater insight and self-knowledge. Have courage and faith in your ability to steadily get through it—and one day you will look back, and see that the black dog was just a shadow in your life. Like a shadow, you have to *look back* to see it—so instead keep *looking forward*!

I feel that I have, through my close shave with death and the enforced learning that followed, learnt to live. I have a new zest for life, and a healthier attitude to my relationships. So it is possible. I'm grateful for my depression, because otherwise I would not have the knowledge and wisdom I now have. Nor would I have met the amazing people I now know. I learnt to live with my depression, and I learnt to live. 'Depression' is such an innocuous word, so unlike the mental torture that it really is. But I know that it is possible not only to live with it, but to come through it, and be truly full of joy.

I put on my fluffy pink bath robe after relaxing in a warm bath scented with rose petals and lavender. Flickering candles cast shadows of freshly picked flowers on the wall. The black dog is asleep on the Persian carpet and I pick up my book to read. Time is precious to me. And although I was lucky that my friends stuck by me through the darkness and did not run away when the going got tough, it was the black dog that brought me to this point. Finally, I have made sense of my depression and it has resulted in my expanded heart. Laughter is impregnated in the walls of this house. Laughter that I thought I had lost and would never regain. I'm not finished living yet, and, in fact, now I'm living as if I'm running out of time.

At first, I tried to scare away the black dog with lots of noise and business and grasped at anything I could to make me feel better, to ease the pain, to disguise myself, to fill up every moment, so that it would not find me. But, after a while, I noticed that it had changed my outlook on life for the better and I came to realise that living with the black dog meant just that, living with the black dog, not trying to kill it off, or run away from it, but looking it squarely in the eye.

I learnt that healing was not about quick cures or even hope, hope that in the future everything would be all right, but about giving the black dog the respect it deserved and internalising the lessons I had been offered. During my worst period, people would say to me 'Things will change', and I'd cry even more for I knew they wouldn't, couldn't . . . Until one day a crisis counsellor said to me, 'No, I agree with you, things may not change, but you will learn to live with your illness'. And finally that made sense.

She was right. I have learnt to live with my illness. Gradually, I discovered I was living with a new consciousness. The black dog had taught me to live every experience as if it were for the last time.

I will use this metaphor; it's as if I was told I was going to lose my eyesight at midnight. No longer would I take my eyesight for granted. I would go outside and stare at the moon or look with intent upon the flowers in the garden. Before depression, I would go to the beach and it was just the beach. I knew there would be plenty of other trips to the beach, so this one didn't matter much. Now when I go to the beach, I take the black dog with me and together we listen to the belly roar of the ocean and her echo in the shells. We taste her salty spray and let ourselves be dumped so we can feel the water in our eyes, nose and ears. We let our bodies ebb and flow like seaweed in the bubbling white foam. At other times, we face her head on, at the last moment giving in to her cold current strength. We wiggle our toes and paws luxuriously in the cool wet sand and breathe in the smell of fish and salty air. We walk backwards along the beach, making mysterious prints in the sand. I do all this because time is of the essence and there may not be beaches where I'm going next.

Zen Buddhists talk of 'beginner's mind', or doing something as if for the first time. Doing things as if for the last time has brought a sweeter fragrance to my life, and it is my supreme gift from the black dog. As well as my new consciousness, I have learnt to control my thinking with cognitive therapy and meditation. I've finally learnt how to be still.

Meditation has helped me to see the true nature of my distractions, my concerns and my attachments, and has let me be as close to my true self as possible without resistance. I learnt through meditating on my losses to diminish my attachments and rebalance my life, and remain mindful that my house, in this lifetime, is made of sticks not bricks. Like many people with depression, I was an overachiever and an obsessive thinker. I focused all of my energy on the building of a career, not realising that it could be taken from me at any moment. Whatever I did, whether it be relationships or work, I invested too much, ignoring the constant of change and the impermanence of existence. Now I make sure I don't put all of my eggs in one basket. As part of my healing, I also began to write a memoir of my life to try and save it. Writing in a journal made me see the absurdity of clinging to rigidity instead of softening and experiencing the reality of my existence. Now, if it's cold, I enjoy the cool air on my skin instead of reaching immediately for something to warm me. If it's hot, I explore the sensation of heat on my skin and savour it.

Depression has taught me so much. I have learnt that, if I allow myself to live long enough, my true face will become clearer and clearer and that it's wrong to kill myself as my spirit will wander forever as a lonesome grey ghost. I have learnt to be compassionate to myself as well as others, but, most importantly, I have learnt to live. And, yes, sometimes I am weary and sometimes nothing appears joyous, but I have learnt to soften to that feeling as well and remain faithful to life.

The other day I caught myself singing 'It's a wonderful life', and I looked over at the black dog in the corner, diminished but not dead. And now when I wake in the night and the black dog is there, I'm not frightened and I don't try to hide, for why would I want to kill that which has taught me to live again—that which has led me to this period of resolution.

24

My 'dark night of the soul' taught me compassion and self-respect. A stronger soul emerged from this experience and I now have a quality of life previously unknown to me. I've realised that I don't have to be perfect and it's not necessary to be liked by everyone.

76

Eventually, gradually, I feel the faint stirring of my mood lifting. It seems too good to be true. The dark clouds slowly dissipate and it seems I am looking at the world properly for the first time. What joy! I feel so relieved and motivated to stay well that I write notes and make real changes in my life to prevent it happening again.

There is nothing pleasant about struggling with depression but I will admit that I have learnt to feel joy and peace in everyday life. Inadvertently, I have probably achieved a low cholesterol level, a low disposition for diabetes and stroke, and a very happy and healthy heart.

I've recently become a volunteer with a mental health organisation. I am lucky enough to be able to travel around to local schools and tell my story in the hope of helping de-stigmatise mental illness in our future generations. After all, it only takes one person to make a difference.

I'm proud of who I am and where I am going. And it doesn't matter how many mistakes I make along the way, because every mistake is just an opportunity to learn something new—and I wouldn't be who I am today if I hadn't made mistakes in the past.

I feel like I have come such a long way in such a short period of time. Through speaking out about my mental illness I have, in fact, been able to find strength within myself to make a difference. Things go wrong for me now and I don't stress or get upset. It's like I've finally been able to accept that life isn't meant to be perfect and that I'm perfect just the way I am. OK, I'm a little bit pudgy, a little bit critical . . . but other than that

I'm pretty alright. I don't hate myself anymore. Well, not all the time—I still have my moments, I still have days when I don't want to get out of bed and face the world. But the difference is that now I can see I'm not a complete failure if I feel this way occasionally. I'm actually quite successful.

It is when I stand up in front of a sea of faces and take that first deep breath before beginning to speak that I look back over what has been and realise just how far I have come. Yes, I have depression—but it doesn't have me. I have successfully tamed my black dog.

309

The black cloud of depression which I had lived with for so long had enriched my life in a totally unexpected way. I developed a core of inner strength that gave me the capability to scale new heights. Also, I developed deep compassion. I realise that I could understand people in a unique way. I had insight into the human condition.

59

Through it, I have learned humbling lessons: I am less angry, less impatient, less driven, less reactive. I have learned to identify what I am feeling and why, and to make choices about my actions. I believe I have become wiser, more compassionate, more open-hearted and spiritually aware due to these depths I have plummeted to, and somehow survived.

492

No one strategy, or 'magic pill' on its own, has been responsible for me coping with depression: it has taken a combination of talking therapy, exercise, diet, the pursuit of gratification, meditation *and* antidepressant medication to transform my life.

In a sense, I have now lost my old self and am in the process of becoming a new person. My experience of living with depression has brought about a heightened awareness. While I am not grateful for having had depression, I accept that I wouldn't be who I am now without having gone through it. Although it does not define me, it's now part of who I am.

I don't know what the future holds for me, but it is much brighter. I take one day at a time now, telling myself that if I'm having a black day then things *will* be better tomorrow.

66

Deep inside, I know I will probably never be fully cured. But I can manage my disease. Instead of my life being a long, dark, relentless sentence, it now takes the form of a journey. It is my life. The choice is mine.

381

I gained a very different perspective on the world. I have a greater appreciation for happiness and affection. I will never again take for granted spending a beautiful day in the sunshine.

385

When you have passed through, you will be richer for your ordeal—ready to truly start living like never before.

348

Beautiful things have been born from my experience—empathy, compassion, strength, openness, power of hope and love.

My experience of depression has given me a greater breadth and depth of emotion than ever before. I am blessed to have this gift.

I choose life, this is my mantra. When I feel the stealth of the black dog creeping up on me, ready to nip at my heels, savage me in my dreams and howl in my heart, I grit my teeth, curl my fists in indignation and repeat this aloud. Choose life. I refuse to let a black dog sink poisonous fangs of melancholy into me; it will nip at my heels and this is unavoidable, but it will never break my skin and bleed life out of me again. I try so hard not to let this happen. This is how I strive to live with depression. I have tasted a sour death, but also the syrupy joy of life: good health, family and friends, dancing, thinking, gratitude and peace. Oh, and how delicious it tastes! I choose life. I have to because I know life is worth living.

558

Everything passes in time. My life, though often dark, has been interesting and rich. In the tapestry of life, dark threads have been as necessary as those of silver and gold.

241

Spending time with the darkness gives me the ability to see things differently. There is a light that burns deep inside me. I have my life ahead of me. It has allowed me to see further inside myself than I could have ever imagined.

591

No matter how alone you feel or how impossible it seems that you will ever be able to feel anything other than complete devastation, realise that you are surrounded by thousands who feel the same and who, in their different ways, know how to help. Use them; the world is better for you in it.

It's only in retrospect that I can feel incredible gratitude for my days of darkness, for the many insights and revelations that are so much a part of who I am and the work I now do. If we can embrace this awakening, we are bound to discover unfathomable joys and profound insights amongst the sadness. Over time, with patience and compassion for ourselves during this process, we can begin to live a more fulfilling and whole life.

This does not mean that the black dog will slink off into the distance, never to return. No, quite the opposite. I suspect the black dog will become a valuable friend, an insightful guide and an important reminder that we are all human, with the capacity for myriad shifting emotions and experiences. If we can embrace the times of darkness with interest and imagination, acknowledge and accept those parts of ourselves that are frightening or appear damaged, there arises an opportunity for deep healing. With this comes the possibility that we might contribute something unique and important to a fellow traveller, enhance our communities in unseen ways, and perhaps create something of value to the world.

395

There is an upside—joy at being alive and a wonderful appreciation for the good things in life. At times, I feel pure exhilaration at being alive and a pulsating sensation from the very forces of life.

288

Depression has changed me. My priorities are clearer. I relish the simple things, learnt to say no, love more deeply, ask for help, look after myself, stay in the moment, live joyfully, learnt to be more courageous and adventurous, and dance around the kitchen. Depression can also be a white dove.

467

My depression made me who I am today and spurred me on to bigger and better things. It makes you who you are and a hell of a lot more individual than most people out there. I still experience life with the same childish awe—perhaps if more adults looked at life this way, the world would be a better place.

342

A mind is like a limb. It can be broken and, even after it mends, it must be cared for with tenderness and compassion. If you have never suffered from depression, you may not know this. In all likelihood, you may have given little thought to the workings of your mind. But serenity is a gift on which too great a value cannot be placed.

Today I do all the things I should to keep my mind strong. I have also learned to relish small joys, the things that are on the surface for us all to see and celebrate. The smile of a stranger, warm sand between my toes, the first tightly-wound buds on my fruit trees, a quiet moment to listen to music or delve into a book.

I avoid noisy or argumentative people, I take the route least likely to be populated by angry drivers, I never do anything just for the money.

I consider depression not a curse, but a wake-up call. It tells you to be true to yourself, to have compassion for yourself as well as others. It leaves a scar that is a reminder of what can be lost and what is worth protecting.

Depression brought my race with myself to a stop. I was forced to look into the darker caves of my conscious. I was scared. I wanted to be like everyone else. I wanted to be normal. But what is normal?

Today I realise that I am like everyone else in one way—I am not impermeable to stress or emotion. But I am grateful that I am different to many in that I have suffered an illness that has made me more accepting of myself and more aware of what I want to strive for. I want a rich life. I want to be wondrously alive and I know that means being wondrously vulnerable.

After a long time, very slowly and quietly, I became aware that a slight 'shift' had occurred. I didn't stumble blinking into the light, but the darkness had less of a hold.

Now I live with less certainty, and I am still finding a place for all my energies (physical, social, intellectual), questioning what it is to live a meaningful life. All experiences change us and leave their mark. But in breaking apart, a life can also be opened. It may take the rest of a lifetime to discover what this means.

It is kindness and simplicity which can help dissolve a sense of separateness and distance from life itself. Sleeping in a newly made bed, having a shower, putting on clean clothes, making and eating something nourishing, speaking to a friend (and being heard), going outside, looking at the sky, a tree, a flower, are small acts of kindness to and for oneself.

Some days even this seemed too much, but there were times when it was possible to put myself in the way of life. Sitting in the garden with a cup of tea I didn't always 'see' what was there, let alone find pleasure in it. Sometimes the 'world' seemed as small as the sensation of warmth from the cup. But there is something insistent about life—and these moments gradually took a stronger hold, and, with this, my attention and appreciation could expand.

Kindness, simplicity, curiosity are all ways of paying attention to what is happening, what questions are being asked, opening up space to consider what is really important. Despite everything, this is a place of opportunity, of possibility.

There are some days when you can see this. There are some days when you can begin to live it. Rather than rushing through life, you might slow down and let it unfold. You could make it up a day at a time.

I wonder, what will happen next?

99

Happiness is evasive. I had to track it down, follow its subtle trail. Pick a bright moment and conjure it in my mind like a magician. Remember, smiling is possible. Hold a torch for it.

Never lose faith, even in the darkest bottom of the deepest pit.

579

Standing up to the black dog has been like a torment from hell. Yet it's so rewarding when the rainbows come in colours far more brilliant than I could ever imagine.

312

It's a miserable existence, suffering over
one's suffering, depressed about one's
depression. It is at these difficult times
that I engrave in my heart and mind:
this WILL pass.

564

Tips from the writers on maintaining wellbeing

- Live one day at a time. Put one foot in front of the other.
- Confront the truth about the black dog's existence. It's not your fault. It just is.
- Be open to suggestions and lifestyle changes. Be passionate about your hobbies.
- Have a dream to aspire to. Accept things you cannot change.
- Affirm yourself as a worthwhile person.
- Feed your spirit with sunshine.
- Read: there is power in knowledge and solace in other worlds and lives.
- Find a tiny glimmer of hope and swim towards it.
- Learn an instrument. Play some music. It may raise your mood and asks nothing in return.
- Recovery begins with understanding. Gaining intimate understanding of your enemy will provide you with weapons to destroy it.
- Appreciate the simple things in life.

- Be aware of the company you keep. Schedule in fun times.
- Recovery requires strength, persistence and hard work. The key to winning the battle is to never give up.
- Just give it time.
- Listen to ABC talks. Grow roses. Keep a cat.
- Never be sorry for yourself.
- Be proactive in your health. Choose to do something positive towards the process of healing, rather than choosing to wallow in negative indulgence.
- Do not rush yourself, or expose yourself to situations you can't handle. You need to recover slowly and gradually emerge from your shell.
- Realise that you aren't alone. Support groups are valuable allies.
- Work towards healing. You must find a way to start—even if you take only small steps. One thing leads to another. Don't expect miracles. Look to the future.
- Write lists of tasks. Plan for your days—this gives something to look forward to, some guiding purpose, a sense of accomplishment.
- Do not go through the journey to wellness alone. Do not rely on one strategy alone.
- Spring clean.
- Breathe.
- Allow backward steps to occur when they must. Deal with the smallest, and only the very next thing. Learn to forgive.
- Savour small moments.

- You can do something. You can make a choice from what seems like nothing.
- Take time out to smell the roses. Create balance and keep everything in moderation. It's also important to be humble.
- It will pass! Both good and bad will pass.
- Always make an effort to do things that have to be done. Do things that you would like to do and things that make you happy. Think positively.
- Recite the litany: *It will pass.*
- Grieve. Allow yourself to be changed by the process.
- Accept that sometimes you will be lonely.
- Have a happy folder filled with things to make you laugh and keep it close by.
- Be grateful. Write down fifteen blessings every day.
- Read *The Tao Te Ching* by Lao-Tzu: it's a relief to read about the 'Great Way' when you have lost your little way.
- Don't dwell on the past. You must move forward and be positive, even though it might be hard.
- When you wake in the morning, the very first words you should say are: *I am not going to accept this mood!* Get motivated. Start with something small, like the dishes.
- Cultivate an attitude of thankfulness, for even the small things.
- The key to getting a grip on the illness is to look beyond it. Forgive yourself your mistakes.
- Recognise that the 'Why me?' attitude will keep you at the mercy of the black dog. Take responsibility for yourself and look for your own answers.

- Concentrate on the present.
- Don't ask why.
- Writing and journalling are healing. All the black dog's howling and muttering remain prisoners of paper and ink.
- Make a list of all the good things you possess and keep it in your pocket.
- Find reassurance in the Buddha's teachings of impermanence—that everything changes.
- Take life fifteen minutes at a time—this is a rule you can use for living.
- Extend towards others. Reach beyond personal woes. Retrain your mind to focus outwardly. Volunteer—it gives you new ideas and distraction. Laugh.
- Join social groups. There are many enjoyable activities and hobbies on offer.
- It's important to celebrate the milestones in your life and realise that time moves ever onwards.
- Don't listen to talk-back radio.
- Don't try to be perfect anymore; simply make the most of what you have.
- Seize the fragments of your day where you have laughter and happiness. Seek it out, go looking for it, let the happiness ooze over you. Recognise that, while depression may never totally disappear, you can learn skills to keep it at bay.
- Realise that nobody can get 'out' of depression—you have to work THROUGH it. It may be a long road ahead.
- Don't read sad stories in newspapers.

- You need structure and meaning to keep in control of depression. It will not simply go away overnight. Control is the key to gaining balance.
- Avoid boredom. Be prepared. Map out a weekly program of activities.
- Don't be a victim.
- Exercise tires out the black dog and makes him sleep.
- Commit yourself to team sports; participating in group activities is something that helps get you out of the house.
- Learn to negotiate the limitations of depression and to push on through, minute by minute, hour by hour, day by day. Set small goals. Occupy yourself. Distract yourself. Be diligent with your skills to manage your illness.
- Learn to accept yourself, for today. Deal with tomorrow, tomorrow.
- There are no quick fixes. You have to commit to staying the course. Realise it's a process of trial and error.
- Formulate an illness plan.
- Do the exact opposite of whatever the black dog says.
- Writing is a way of being WITH YOURSELF—a way to be present with the profound anguish.
- The most important thing is that YOU take action.
- Realise when you need to take time out. Meditation is a great comfort.
- You have to trust it's a temporary condition. You can travel through it.
- Pray for strength.
- Listening to others and supporting them to make changes may get you out of your own head.

- Sometimes you have to live with the hand life deals you.
- Do not set deadlines for your healing.
- Become less rigid and more flexible in your thinking. Make the word 'should' disappear from your vocabulary. Self-acceptance opens the door to a much more fulfilling life.
- Do not look forward or backward. Remain in the clarity of the present moment, in that ephemeral space between the past and the future.
- Life is made up of many moments and many days, some precious, others less so. Try not to be so hard on yourself; let yourself simply 'be'.
- Become proactive. Get out of the house for a change of scenery. Sit in the sun. Go for a walk. Live a more active lifestyle. Help others. Find pleasure. Develop an interest. Keep up your personal appearance.
- Be willing to 'do the hard yards'.
- Create mental 'snapshots' of good times to look back on.
- Find your solace, whatever that may be, and cultivate it. Make especially sure that you enjoy it when times are good. Then, when times are bad, it will be there for your comfort.

Afterword

The Black Dog Institute's Consumer & Community team has hosted a popular writing competition since 2004. The inaugural competition invited people to investigate the origins of the term 'black dog' as a descriptor for depression. While Winston Churchill popularised the evocative metaphor, it had strong antecedents running back many centuries. The response was outstanding and this rich history was published (Eyers, 2006).

Our Institute's name also respects this image. Our logo, brilliantly designed by John Bevins, has the 'V for Victory' in the foreground reflecting the aim set by all clinicians and researchers to be victorious over depression. However, with the 'V' creating the shadow of the black dog, we are reminded of the reality, that depression still shadows the sufferer and needs vigilant management.

The Institute's second writing competition called on people with mood disorders, as well as their family members and friends to describe how they live with the black dog and attracted over six hundred entries.

Why did so many people take the time to write?

They may have wanted to reach into another's darkness and hold forth a light. They may believe that in helping to illuminate even one person's life, their own pain would have more value and meaning. They may have written in the hope of saving someone else from days, months or years of anguish.

> I wish to be an ambassador for this despicable disease. If I can save one life by raising awareness, then it's worth it.

Hopefully what you have read will help you and others along the way. Perhaps you have found some knowledge and wisdom needed to negotiate depression's terrain. Perhaps the stories have helped dispel feelings of fear, stigma or shame, and inspired the perspective needed to continue the fight.

Recognise that you are not alone. There is hope. There is 'light at the end of the tunnel'. The black dog of depression can be brought to heel.

THIS TOO WILL PASS

Where to from here?

The Black Dog Institute is an educational, research, clinical and community-oriented facility, dedicated to improving understanding, diagnosis and treatment of mood disorders.

Our website is a resource targeted to the needs of consumers, carers, students and health professionals, providing a useful stepping stone in the search for quality information about depression and bipolar disorder. On the website can be found:

- A list of emergency helplines.
- Fact Sheets, providing information on types, causes, symptoms and treatments of depression and bipolar disorder.
- Self-tests for depression, postnatal depression and bipolar disorder.
- Information on what to expect from a mental health consultation, where to seek help and what to do if you're not getting better.
- Access to the online Bipolar Disorder Education Program.
- Lists of recommended websites and books.

- Information on the Consumer and Community Resource Centre, including details of public events, lending library and support groups.
- Information on our clinical services, Community Education and Outreach programs, and Education and Training courses for professionals.
- The judges' selection of three winning entries and twelve highly commended awards for the 2006 writing competition are also available to download.

www.blackdoginstitute.org.au

Glossary

Acute   Used to refer to the rapid and recent onset of an illness—commonly severe and intense—which might improve or proceed to a more chronic state.

Affective disorder/illness   The group of psychiatric disorders where a mood disturbance is the first-ranking condition. Thus, a person with depression experiences a persisting very low mood, whereas a person with bipolar disorder is hampered by both very low and very elevated (hypomanic or manic) mood states.

'Bipolar' or bipolar disorder   Bipolar disorder—once called manic depressive illness—is an affective disorder characterised by episodes of mania ('highs') or hypomania alone, or with depressive episodes ('lows') at other times. It is now subdivided into Bipolar I and Bipolar II disorder.

Bipolar I   This involves episodes of mania and depression, so that the 'highs' are generally more severe, last longer and may be associated with delusions and/or hallucinations.

Bipolar II   This involves episodes of both hypomania and depression (but no experience of mania).

Bipolar depression   This is an episode of depression in an individual with bipolar disorder. It is severe, and almost invariably melancholic or psychotic.

Chronic   When an illness has continued for a long time.

'Clinical' depression   An episode of depression that has been present for most of the day for two weeks or more, and is sufficiently severe in its expression and is associated with impaired functioning (at home or at work).

Cognitive behavioural therapy (CBT)   CBT is a technique that attempts to alleviate depression by providing 'tools' to help examine the truth of everyday assumptions and interpretations, as some people with depression often have a negative view of themselves (even when not depressed), and develop entrenched thinking patterns that are so habitual that they don't notice their irrational judgement.

Consumer   A title adopted by users of goods and services, and in this context used to refer to a person who has used or is currently using mental health services to achieve improved mental health. Its intent is to empower people as against referring to them as 'patients'.

Counselling   Counselling involves listening, empathy and helping the client to structure and make sense of their experience. Finding solutions to personal problems can be of benefit to those with a personality style that has a leaning towards depression.

Delusional depression   This is also termed psychotic depression. The person experiences false beliefs (delusions) during a depressive episode, and/or false perceptions (hallucinations).

Depression   Depression is a broad term that can encompass normal mood states, clinical syndromes and actual disease states (e.g. melancholia). At the 'clinical depression' level, it involves body, mood and thoughts, and affects a person's view of themselves. Symptoms include loss of interest and pleasure; loss of appetite; weight loss or gain; loss of emotional expression; a persistently sad, anxious or empty mood; feelings of hopelessness, pessimism, guilt, worthlessness or helplessness; social withdrawal; and unusual fatigue and low energy.

A depressive disorder is not the same as a passing 'blue mood'. It is not a sign of personal weakness or a condition that can be wished away. Without treatment, symptoms can last for weeks, months or years. Appropriate treatment, however, can help most people with depression.

Depressogenic event   This is the term for a stressful life event (e.g. loss of job, serious family dispute) that is likely to have caused or precipitated depression, or, in a person with bipolar disorder, depression or hypo/mania.

Diurnal variation   This is a change in depressive mood and energy level at certain times of the day. In general, those with melancholic depression report their mood and energy as worse in the morning, those with non-melancholic depression describe the opposite, and those with psychotic depression report no diurnal variation.

Electroconvulsive therapy (ECT) ECT is a modern psychiatric treatment that is effective across a narrow range of psychiatric disorders, not only melancholic and psychotic depression but also (though rarely used) in the treatment of manic disorders and certain types of schizophrenia. It has been established as the most effective antidepressant treatment available for melancholic and psychotic depression, and is a therapeutic option if other usually beneficial treatments for those conditions have been unsuccessful. Research has shown that more than 80 per cent of patients who have had ECT are willing to receive the treatment again.

Endogenous depression An older term for melancholic depression, reflecting the view that such depression was not related to stress but came, more, from the individual.

Episode This refers to a bout of depression. To qualify as 'clinical' depression, the episode should be present for most of the day for two weeks or more.

General practitioner (GP) A general practitioner is a medical doctor who provides primary care. A GP treats acute and chronic illnesses, and provides preventive care and health education for all age groups.

'High' This is the term used for the abnormal upswing in mood that is characteristic of hypomania or mania.

Hypomania   A 'high' that is less severe than the highs of a manic episode, and without any psychotic features.

Kindling   The effect observed when an affective illness starts out as 'reactive' and then over time becomes 'endogenous', taking on a life of its own—with episodes often emerging without any preceding clear stressor. The brain is a highly regulated system with a lot of feedback loops, and if it is stressed then rested then stressed again repeatedly, it can become increasingly sensitised to such stress.

Major depression   This is a diagnostic term describing an episode of depression, with five or more specific features (e.g. depressed mood, loss of interest and pleasure, sleep disturbance) that is present for two weeks or more, and associated with social impairment.

Mania   A high mood of distinct severity where, commonly, the individual is psychotic (has lost touch with reality) and is experiencing delusions and hallucinations.

Melancholia/melancholic depression   This is the biological depressive subtype that is likely to emerge without any clearly explanatory antecedent stressors and which has distinct clinical features, such as slowed movement and non-reactive mood. It has genetic causes. It responds to physical treatments such as medications, and sometimes ECT is a necessary treatment.

Mood   This is a personal description of how an individual feels (contrasting with 'affect', or how the individual appears), or a reference to a more persistent emotional state than an affect.

Physical treatment   A term used for a treatment that is designed to modify biological processes (e.g. medication or ECT) as opposed to psychological interventions which focus on the psychological world of the individual.

Postnatal depression   Any type of depression in a mother in the first 12 months following the birth of her baby.

Primary and secondary conditions   The word 'primary' as in 'primary depression' indicates that the condition 'stands alone'. Secondary depression generally indicates that the depression follows, or is otherwise related to, another major medical condition, whether psychiatric (e.g. anxiety disorder), medical (e.g. a stroke) or other primary factor (e.g. alcohol abuse).

Psychosis   Impairment of mental functioning in which the individual loses touch with reality and usually experiences delusions and/or hallucinations.

Psychotherapy   This is a non-physical treatment in which the therapist adopts a particular structure (e.g. analytic, interpersonal, cognitive, cognitive behavioural) to address symptoms and/or personality problems experienced by an individual.

Psychotic depression   Severe depression with the added presence of psychotic symptoms, that is, delusions and hallucinations.

Relapse   The return of a full episode of depression when the individual has not completely recovered from an earlier episode.

Side-effects   Unintended effects of medication that can exist alongside any positive effects of the drug; more discernible in the older-style antidepressants. Side-effects are usually most pronounced in the first few weeks of treatment, but others (e.g. weight gain, thyroid dysfunction) may appear after a period.

Stigma   A sense of shame felt by people as they attempt to fulfil their accustomed roles in the face of discrimination by the wider community.

Stressor   An event or interpersonal interaction that causes distress. Stressors can be acute (e.g. the immediate aftermath of an accident) or chronic (e.g. poverty, a poor marriage).

References

Bakowski, P. 1995, 'Counsel', from *In the Human Night*, Hale & Iremonger, Sydney, p. 69. Extract reproduced with permission.

Descartes, R. 1952, from 'Discourse on the method of rightly conducting the reasoning, Part 4', in *Great Books of the Western World, Vol. 3: Descartes, Spinoza*, ed. R.M. Hutchins, Encyclopaedia Britannica Inc., William Benton, Chicago, p. 51.

Eliot, T.S. 1995, 'Quartet 1: Burnt Norton', *Four Quartets*, Faber and Faber, London, p. 5.

Eyers, K. (ed.) 2006, *Tracking the Black Dog: Hairy tales and historical legwork from the Black Dog Institute's Writing Competition*, UNSW Press, Sydney.

Gallop, G. 2006, Press release. Statement from the Premier of Western Australia. Content authorised by the Government Media Office, Department of the Premier and Cabinet, 16 January.

H.H. The Dalai Lama and Cutler, H.C. 2003, *The Art of Happiness. A Handbook for Living*, Hodder Headline, Sydney.

Jamison, K. 1995, *An Unquiet Mind: A Memoir of Moods and Madness*, Alfred A. Knopf, New York.

Johnstone, M., 2005, *I Had a Black Dog*, Pan MacMillan, Sydney.

Karp, D. 1996, *Speaking of Sadness: Depression, Disconnection, and the Meanings of Illness*, Oxford University Press, New York.

———2001, *The Burden of Sympathy: How families cope with mental illness*, Oxford University Press, New York.

Kibby, L. 1989, 'The Traveller', from *Insights, Spiritual Awareness and Human Be-ing*, independently published and distributed, Victoria, p. 27. Extract reproduced with permission.

King, P. 2004, *Your Life Matters: The Power of Living Now*, Random House, Sydney, p. 52.

Lao-Tzu, translated by Lau, D.C. 2001, *The Tao Te Ching*, Chinese University Press, The Chinese University of Hong Kong.

Leunig, M. 2005, 'A most depressing thing occurs ...'. Poem published in *The Age*, 12 May, ID # 117024056. Extract reproduced with permission.

MHA (Mental Health Association): http://www.mental health. asn.au (Australia); http://www.nmha.org/ (America); http:// www.mind.org.uk (United Kingdom).

Razer, H. 1999, *Gas Smells Awful: The Mechanics of Being a Nutcase*, Random House, Sydney.

Robbins, A. 2001, *Awaken the Giant Within*, Pocket Books, Simon & Schuster Inc., London, p. 82.

Styron, W. 1990, *Darkness Visible*, Random House, New York.

Voltaire, (Francois Marie Arouet), quoted in de Beauvoir, S., 1972, *Old Age* (trans. Patrick O'Brian), Penguin Books, Harmondsworth, p. 337.

Dealing With Depression
A common sense guide to mood disorders
by Gordon Parker

'This unique book, written by one of the world's leading authorities on depression, focuses on a way of thinking about the complexity and diversity of the mood disorders that is both easy to understand and 'rings' true. Well-written and thought provoking, it is essential reading for all whose lives are affected by depression.'

Michael Thase, Professor of Psychiatry, University of Pittsburgh

Most of us get 'the blues' at some point in our lives, and some people find that they just can't shake them. How can you tell when you or someone you know is suffering from depression that needs clinical treatment? How can you find the best treatment for your depression?

Dealing With Depression is a brief, user-friendly guide to depression and mood disorders for sufferers, their families, and health professionals who care for them. Professor Parker explains that contrary to popular belief, there are many different types of depression, each benefiting from differing treatments.

He outlines the advantages and disadvantages of drug and non-drug treatments, and offers advice on matching the different types of depression with their most appropriate treatment. He shows that while depression may be severe and disabling, it can be treated successfully providing it is diagnosed and managed properly.

Covering everything from a typical 'blue mood' to severe clinical depression, including mood states such as bipolar disorder, *Dealing With Depression* is one of the most comprehensive and accessible guides available for the general reader and health professional.

ISBN 978 1 74114 214 3